Advanced Information and Knowledge Processing

SpringerBriefs in Advanced Information and Knowledge Processing

Series Editors

Xindong Wu, School of Computing and Informatics, University of Louisiana at Lafayette, Lafayette, LA, USA

Lakhmi Jain, University of Technology Sydney, Sydney, NSW, Australia

T0171963

SpringerBriefs in Advanced Information and Knowledge Processing presents concise research in this exciting field. Designed to complement Springer's *Advanced Information and Knowledge Processing* series, this Briefs series provides researchers with a forum to publish their cutting-edge research which is not yet mature enough for a book in the *Advanced Information and Knowledge Processing* series, but which has grown beyond the level of a workshop paper or journal article. Typical topics may include, but are not restricted to:

Big Data analytics
Big Knowledge
Bioinformatics
Business intelligence
Computer security
Data mining and knowledge discovery
Information quality and privacy
Internet of things
Knowledge management
Knowledge-based software engineering
Machine intelligence
Ontology
Semantic Web
Smart environments
Soft computing
Social networks

SpringerBriefs are published as part of Springer's eBook collection, with millions of users worldwide and are available for individual print and electronic purchase. Briefs are characterized by fast, global electronic dissemination, standard publishing contracts, easy-to-use manuscript preparation and formatting guidelines and expedited production schedules to assist researchers in distributing their research fast and efficiently.

More information about this subseries at http://www.springer.com/series/16024

Rae Earnshaw · John Dill · David Kasik

Data Science and Visual Computing

 Springer

Prof. Rae Earnshaw
Faculty of Engineering and Informatics
Centre for Visual Computing
University of Bradford
Bradford, UK

Visiting Fellow
St John's College University of Durham
Durham, UK

Visiting Professor
Faculty of Arts, Science and Technology
Wrexham Glyndwr University
Wrexham, UK

Mr. David Kasik
Boeing Senior Technical Fellow Emeritus
Visualization and Interactive Techniques
Sammamish, WA, USA

Prof. John Dill
School of Interactive Arts and Technology
Simon Fraser University—Surrey Campus
Surrey, BC, Canada

ISSN 1610-3947   ISSN 2197-8441   (electronic)
Advanced Information and Knowledge Processing
ISSN 2524-5198   ISSN 2524-5201   (electronic)
SpringerBriefs in Advanced Information and Knowledge Processing
ISBN 978-3-030-24366-1   ISBN 978-3-030-24367-8   (eBook)
https://doi.org/10.1007/978-3-030-24367-8

This Springer imprint is published by the registered company Springer Nature Switzerland AG
The registered company address is: Gewerbestrasse 11, 6330 Cham, Switzerland

The authors dedicate this book to their parents, partners, and to the memory of Jim Thomas.

Foreword

Rae Earnshaw was one of the first two scholars to graduate with a Ph.D. in computer graphics from a UK university and has followed his passion for technology ever since. I know this because I was the other one! Rae started exploring fundamental algorithms for CAD in the 1970s and has moved with the times publishing many research papers on the cutting edge. With his talent for organization, he brought together groups of researchers under the auspices of a series of NATO Institutes. I remember in the 1980s meeting such luminaries as Jack Bresenham, Maureen Stone, Kees van Overveld, and Roy Hall, researchers who have had significant influence on the field of computer graphics.

Professor Emeritus John Dill came to Simon Fraser University (SFU) from a senior position in industry in 1987. He moved to the School of Interactive Arts and Technology from SFU's School of Engineering Science in 2005, and has worked in the fields of Computer Graphics, Computer-Aided Design, Information Visualization, Human–Computer Interaction and, most recently, Visual Analytics (VA). John Dill was a member of the US National Visual Analytics Centre panel that defined VA and contributed to the well-cited VA bible: "Illuminating the Path". In 2016, Dill was awarded the IEEE Visualization Career Award.

Boeing Senior Technical Fellow, David Kasik, was also a pioneer of VA. Dill and colleagues received a directed gift from the Boeing Company, to establish the SFU-based Vancouver Institute for Visual Analytics, a joint SFU-UBC effort. Aircraft present a data nightmare to visualize and track the thousands of parts. David Kasik developed computer-aided design software, 3D viewing software, and pioneered the use of visual analytics. This gave Boeing the ability to view over a billion geometric polygons on commodity hardware, and VA helps extract more information from complex non-geometric data. David is an ACM Fellow, an IEEE Distinguished Scientist, and in 2012 he received the ACM Siggraph Outstanding Service Award.

Finding a needle in a haystack is a difficult, if not impossible, assignment. This is the problem we encounter when trying to extract information and meaning from the increasingly large amounts of data being generated in many disciplines. Computer graphics has long been involved in handling large amounts of data in areas such as

CAD/CAM, scientific data analysis, simulations, animations, and special effects for movies. More recently, attention has been given to VA where greater consideration is given to the interaction of the user with data in order to explore possible areas of interest, and to directly link the analytical reasoning power of the human with the visual information spaces of the data.

An ACM Siggraph Panel in 1988 on "*Pretty Pictures are not so Pretty anymore*" chaired by Rae Earnshaw (with panellists Jack Bresenham, David Dobkin, Robin Forrest, and Leo Guibas) advanced a thesis from a NATO Advanced Study Institute [1] that images needed to go beyond ultra-realism and give more attention to the foundation objectives of computer graphics. It could be argued that visual analytics is partly an example of this. A joint European Union/National Science Foundation initiative in 1999 sought to define the research objectives in the areas of virtual environments and human–computer interaction [2]. The latter aspect, and the importance of human cognition, is particularly important for visual analytics.

Big data can arise in the context of a variety of application areas. This volume highlights these areas and the strategies currently being adopted nationally and internationally to address the challenging and complex issues that are involved in analyzing very large datasets.

The co-authors bring a wealth of expertise and long experience in this subject area. In fact, because their careers are linked through their pioneering efforts in the fields of computer graphics and visualization, these authors are well placed to develop the important themes of the relationship between data science and visual tools. In this way, computer graphics and visualization can have direct real-world benefits. They are not just pretty pictures!

December 2018   Brian Wyvill
                                                                              Canada Research Chair
                                                                             University of Victoria
                                                                                 Victoria, BC, Canada

References

1. Earnshaw, R.A. (ed.): Theoretical Foundations of Computer Graphics and CAD, F40, pp. 1270. Springer-Verlag, (1988). ISBN: 3-540-19506-8. https://link.springer.com/book/10.1007/978-3-642-83539-1
2. Brown, J.R., van Dam A., Earnshaw R.A., Encarnacao J.L., Guedj, R.A.: Special report on human-centered computing, online communities and virtual environments. ACM SIGGRAPH Computer Graphics, 33(3), 42–62 (1999). online at http://www.siggraph.org/publications/newsletter/v33n3/contributions/special.html

Preface

This book presents an analysis of the fields of data science and visual computing. It also explains the key elements and drivers in these fields. Visual tools are becoming increasingly important due to the large amounts of data produced by a variety of digital processes. These include scientific experiments, remote sensors, simulations, monitoring of business processes, security data, social media, and recording devices. There are also more invisible forms of data such as that being transmitted and received within the context of the Internet of Things. Global data are increasingly complex and heterogeneous, and are predicted to rise to over 100 zettabytes (where one zettabyte is one trillion gigabytes) by 2025 [1], which is a tenfold increase in the current volume of worldwide data. Such data are widely accepted as being strategically important to the operation and positioning of businesses, which has given rise to the many external and internal data monitoring procedures, such as dashboards or gallery displays, now used routinely by companies to show key performance indicators and other data. It is also widely accepted as being mandatory for a greater understanding of data from medical sensors and imaging, and of global processes such as weather forecasting. It is also expected to become increasingly relevant to the normal routines of human life in areas, where digital transactions are performed such as electronic banking and online commodity purchasing, and in national and global areas such as food production and border controls. Although the issues of data storage, management, and access can be handled by the cloud, a more important issue is to understand what is contained in the data and its significance.

In the Foreword to a book by Earnshaw and Wiseman [2], Dr. James Clark (then Chairman of Silicon Graphics Inc.) expressed this as follows: *"Virtually all comprehension in science, technology and even art calls on our ability to visualize. In fact, the ability to visualize is almost synonymous with understanding. We have all used the expression 'I see' to mean 'I understand'"*. This initial quest for understanding was driven by the developments of fast 3D hardware and realistic image generation and was particularly successful in areas such as the analysis of scientific data, computer-aided design, simulations, and the production of special effects sequences for films. Thus, the primary focus at that time was in the processing and outputting of information in visual form. However, the linking of visualization with understanding was very far-sighted because this has continued to be the driving force behind the interactive analysis of today's very large and complex datasets. This was also expressed in a similar way by Hamming [3] as: *"the purpose of computing is insight not numbers"*. Therefore, the objective of the analysis is to provide an understanding of, and insight into, the meaning of the data.

Visual representations capitalize on the bandwidth of the human visual system and maximize the power of human reasoning and cognition in order to be able to extract validated meaning and knowledge from data. The range and volume of data sources have increased enormously over time, particularly those generating real-time data. This has posed additional challenges for the management and analysis of the data and also its effective representation and display. A wide range of application areas are able to benefit from the latest visual tools and facilities. These include all areas of science and engineering, life sciences, and the arts and humanities. Rapid analysis is needed in areas where immediate decisions need to be made based on the results of the analysis of the data. Such areas include weather forecasting, stock exchange, epidemiology, and security threats. In areas where the volume of data being produced far exceeds the current capacity to analyze all of it, attention is being focussed on how best to address these challenges.

Computer hardware and software have diversified since the early days of visualization. In particular, they have become ubiquitous through the increasing power and capability of graphics cards for personal computers and the availability of excellent graphics facilities on low-cost computers and mobile devices such as phones and tablets. However, hardware and software of itself may not necessarily lead to a better understanding of the data. Equally important are data selection, data representation, and the effect of the information on the human's cognitive processes. This volume examines all these areas and explains why they are significant.

This volume is in the SpringerBriefs series, and its objective therefore is to provide a summary of the fields of data science and visual computing. This is achieved by detailing the higher level concepts and paradigms that govern the area; presenting the latest developments in the hardware and software available; providing the latest information on business application areas; and summarizing the latest results in research and development. The authors have been closely involved in the fields of data science and visual computing since their inception and have designed and used some of the tools and environments used to explore data and analyze information, as well as the interfaces to such tools and applications.

There is insufficient space in a brief book of this nature to provide full details on any particular area and, where relevant, the more detailed material in the Further Reading and References at the end of each chapter are for the reader to "drill down" and gain more information where they feel they need it. The References concentrate on recent years as these represent the latest developments and advances, and these are probably of most interest and relevance to readers. Some older references are included where they detail significant pioneering advances in the field in earlier years. The Further Reading includes some references which are more tutorial or review in nature and these contain further lists of key references throughout the time frame of the development of the particular subject area.

Therefore this review of data science and visual computing is very much a "bird's eye view" of the field. There is only space therefore to review those areas in the public domain where it is felt that some of the key developments are taking place. The nature of these developments is presented, but not the technical detail. The reader is therefore referred to the Further Reading and the References for this detail. It should be noted that military applications have access to specialized facilities for accessing and processing large amounts of data, and these methods are not accessible to the public for security reasons. In addition, large multi-national corporations have their own very large databases (e.g., of customer preferences) which they use for their own business purposes. They have state-of-the-art methods for analysis of their data and the extraction of information relevant for their businesses. For commercial reasons, such methods are not normally in the public domain.

Where the references are to online papers and documents, the authors have endeavored to provide those that are open source and in the public domain rather than behind a paywall. The current move to a requirement for open-source publication in Europe will assist this situation in the future (on the basis that the taxpayer has already contributed to the funding of research and development and therefore should be entitled to read the publications without further charge). Where publications are currently behind a paywall, readers can normally read the abstract and see the list of references before deciding whether to purchase the paper.

Each chapter in this volume contains the main points in the area and the reasons for their significance. It is not intended to examine each of these points in detail—there is insufficient space to do this. However, the interested reader can follow up in the Further Reading or References for further detail and information. There is also a summary at the front of the chapter (rather longer than usual) to set out what is covered in the chapter.

There are many references to online sources on the Internet. Readers of the e-book can access these directly as they are embedded in the text as hot links. Some URLs of web pages change over time due to site names being changed by their owners, or the position of the website in the site hierarchy being changed. Where the link does not access the required page, the correct page can often be located by putting the URL into Google. If this doesn't work due to Google's cached copy of the original website having been overwritten, then the title of the reference can be typed into Google.

It is hoped that this book makes a useful contribution to an important area of significant ongoing research, development, and application.

Bradford/Durham/Wrexham, UK   Rae Earnshaw
Surrey, Canada   John Dill
Sammamish, USA   David Kasik
April 2019

References

1. Cave, A.: What will we do when the world's data hits 163 zettabytes. In: 2025? (2017). https://www.forbes.com/sites/andrewcave/2017/04/13/what-will-we-do-when-the-worlds-data-hits-163-zettabytes-in-2025/#45e8626349ab
2. Earnshaw, R.A., Wiseman, N.: An Introductory Guide to Scientific Visualization. Springer, Berlin Heidelberg (1992). https://www.springer.com/gb/book/9783642634703, https://link.springer.com/book/10.1007/978-3-642-58101-4
3. Hamming, R.W.: Numerical Methods for Scientists and Engineers, Dover Publications Inc., Mineola, NY (first published 1962) (1987). http://store.doverpublications.com/0486652416.html

Acknowledgements

Thanks and appreciations are due to all those who read draft versions of the chapters and provided comments to improve technical content and readability. However, responsibility for the final text rests with the authors.

Thanks are expressed to Prof. Brian Wyvill for providing the Foreword to the book.

Thanks and appreciations are also due to Springer for assistance and support with the editing and production of this book.

Bradford/Durham/Wrexham, UK   Rae Earnshaw
Surrey, Canada   John Dill
Sammamish, USA   David Kasik
April 2019

Contents

Chapter 1
Data Science

Rae Earnshaw

Abstract Data science seeks to define and implement methods and procedures to extract information and knowledge from datasets. Computer algorithms need data to produce results. Given the early developments of hardware to perform the required calculations, the initial focus was on providing software to interface to the requirements of the user. As the power of the hardware increased, larger amounts of output were produced. At the same time, the transition to increasing use of the Internet and mobile computing has generated a much wider variety of data types. This complexity of data has generated an increasing requirement for specialized software tools and environments to provide the processing and analysis required. The objective is to understand the meaning of complex datasets. Business and commerce wish to know how their products and services meet the current and future requirements of the market place, as well as understanding the meaning of data that is internal to their own organizations. The rise of data science is due principally to the need to analyze large and complex datasets with high-value content. Such techniques are increasingly utilizing machine learning and artificial intelligence to provide effective ways forward.

Keywords Data processing · Visual processing machine · Machine learning · Data mining · Data warehousing · Fire-hoses of data · Complexity of data · Unstructured data · Data protection

1.1 Introduction

Data and its analysis are fundamental to the computational process. Such data may be external or internal to the computer. Internal data may be generated for the purposes of simulation using a computer-based model of some external process. External data can come from a variety of sources: somewhere, the data is specified by humans and others where it is automatically generated from monitoring devices such as experiments, sensors, and video cameras, or data acquisition equipment such as micro-

© The Author(s), under exclusive license to Springer Nature Switzerland AG 2019   1
R. Earnshaw et al., *Data Science and Visual Computing*,
SpringerBriefs in Advanced Information and Knowledge Processing,
https://doi.org/10.1007/978-3-030-24367-8_1

scopes and telescopes. Data is processed by the computer according to algorithms which specify the analyses to be performed. New data is output which is the result of the computation. Thus computer processing has generated new information which in turn may be regarded as a contribution to knowledge.

The history of computing illustrates continuous hardware and software developments delivering increased processing speeds and reducing costs, alongside a greater variety of devices and options for data storage, whether local or in the Cloud [1, 2]. The earliest application areas for computer processing were in science and engineering due to the numerical orientation of the original data, but over time have widened significantly to include all disciplines and types of business. Therefore, the volume and variety of data sources have increased over time, and the demand for effective computer processing remains undiminished. In parallel with this, data and services have increasingly migrated to the Cloud for ease of access and use.

1.2   Defining Data Science

Data science uses scientific methods, processes, algorithms, and systems to extract insights and information from data [3]. It is important to be able to perform rigorous and reliable analysis when decisions are to be made based on the results of analyzing the data [4]. When the datasets are unstructured, supplementary processes are needed to structure the data in order to analyze it. Unstructured data which contains different types of data can occur in many applications areas such as social media and web data. The upsurge in interest in data science has been principally brought about by a number of factors, including the following:

(i)   increasing digitization and data collection processes that have generated more data;

(ii)   increasing volumes and complexity of data which require analysis for scientific or business reasons;

(iii)   the large amounts of computer power now available, either locally or via the cloud;

(iv)   the increasing sophistication of software that is available; and

(v)   the increasing speed and capacity of the Internet, allowing connecting a large variety of devices in addition to typical computing devices, such as thermostats, refrigerators, and automobiles. This is referred to as the "Internet of Things" (IoT).

Data science includes the related areas of machine learning and data mining. Machine learning may be regarded as a subfield of artificial intelligence and enables a computer program to draw conclusions from a dataset based on inference or patterns in the data. Data mining uses machine learning and statistical methods to uncover areas of interest in large datasets. Commercial interests in data mining are high because companies in competitive situations want to know how best to utilize any information they gain about the interests of their customers, and also the market place for their products and services. The term data science is often used to include all areas to do with the capturing and processing of data including cleaning, warehousing, and converting unstructured data to structured data—before its subsequent analysis and output of results. Of special relevance to this latter aspect is how to optimally present the results of the analysis in order to accurately convey its meaning and significance, particularly when there are large volumes of data to display.

The transition from the early computers to the Internet and mobile computing has brought about a substantial increase in the varieties of data and also their volume. This includes emails, podcasts, blogs, web searches, video uploads and downloads, photographs, images, e-books, online video games, audio files, and online shopping. All these represent potential markets which advertisers wish to exploit. The number of Internet users increased from 3.6 billion in 2017 to 3.9 billion in 2018, and has almost quadrupled from 2005 [5], and will continue to increase in the future—producing still more data. Figure 1.1 shows the number of Internet users per 100 inhabitants from 1997 to 2018.

The trends for producing more data in all its varieties increases the strategic importance of being able to understand real-time trends in the data in order to evaluate the predictive aspects. What will be the possible future interests and buying requirements

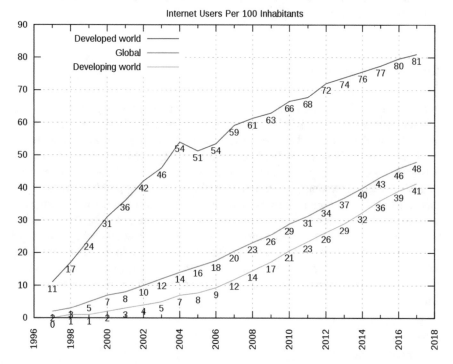

Fig. 1.1 The number of Internet users per 100 inhabitants from 1997 to 2018. Courtesy of Wikipedia https://en.m.wikipedia.org/wiki/Global_Internet_usage. Content made available by CC BY-SA 3.0. https://creativecommons.org/licenses/by-sa/3.0/

of online users? How can future advertising be targeted to capture their interests? Clearly, business and commerce are keen to obtain answers to these questions.

1.3   Visual Data

Input and output data may be alphanumeric or visual images. Output data which contains graphical representations rather than a table of numbers may enable a human to more fully comprehend the significance of the data. As noted by Hamming:

> *"The purpose of computing is insight not numbers"* [6] and by Gross:

> Among our sensory channels, the visual path is the most important one, and large parts of our brain are allocated to it. For this reason, visual representation and analysis of information is a natural process for human beings and thus extremely efficient on any kind of data base [7].

This introduces the concept of visual computing, where the computer may be regarded as a visual processing machine. This includes processing of image data where this is input to the computer, and a faithful and appropriate visual representation for data that is to be output. Image processing is often considered part of the overall process of data visualization.

1.4   Visualization of Data

In the 1970s and 80s, supercomputers were increasingly producing "fire-hoses" of data representing the results of numerical calculations. This resulted in incoming data being warehoused as there was insufficient time to analyze and display it. In 1986, the National Science Foundation in the USA requested an investigation as to how graphics and image processing hardware and software could be utilized within the NSF-funded supercomputer centers in order to address this problem. An analysis was performed by representatives from the academy, industry, and government, and the report "Visualization in Scientific Computing" was produced [8]. The principal recommendations were to provide investment in research and technology developments in the area of tools for scientific visualization, for both the short and long terms. Improved tools were seen as essential for the processing and display of large datasets. Visualization was regarded as drawing on research and development in the following fields:

- Computer graphics,
- Image processing,
- Computer vision,
- Computer-aided design,
- Signal processing, and
- User interface studies.

Although this initiative was largely driven by data analysis requirements in science and engineering, it is now widely accepted that such tools and interfaces can be applied equally in all disciplines and applications, in particular, to data sources where there is no "natural" underlying geometry, as is the case for engineering and science. Tools of course may be customized for particular application domains.

Moves to large data centers have focussed attention on using the data center as a computer [9].

1.5 Commercial Research and Development

Deriving optimum strategies for dealing with very large datasets has now moved principally to commercial organizations as they have their own proprietary databases on which to develop and test their algorithms to extract information and knowledge. Their databases are continually increasing in size due to the data which is being accumulated in real time from their users, thus potentially increasing the sophistication of the algorithms they develop. Such companies include Google, Facebook, Amazon, Instagram, Microsoft, Apple, and Spotify. The size of such databases is not in the public domain but is estimated to be billions of terabytes. Such companies record every mouse click and every web page that is browsed in order to be able to obtain a picture of the interests and behaviors of the billions of people who use such facilities on the Internet. They are able to sell such information to the highest bidder, who in turn are able to optimally target their advertising to user interests. Table 1.1 summarizes key data for the major companies, and Table 1.2 key data for social media companies.

Table 1.1 indicates the dominant position that the major companies have in the market place.

Data in Tables 1.1 and 1.2 courtesy of the following sources:
https://www.statista.com/
https://www.forbes.com/

Table 1.1 Key data for major companies (as at 2019). Numbers are approximate

Company	Number of users	Market share	Revenue (p.a.)	Employees	Founded
Google	1 billion	90%	$150 billion	100,000	1998
Facebook	2 billion	66%	$60 billion	30,000	2004
Amazon	>300 million (100 million Prime)	45%	$250 billion	650,000	1994
Microsoft	1.2 billion (Office)	75% (Windows)	$100 billion	135,000	1975
Apple	600 million (1 billion devices)	12% (OSX)	$270 billion	132,000	1976

Table 1.2 Key data for social media companies

Company	Number of users	Market share (%)	Revenue (p.a.)	Employees	Founded
Instagram (owned by Facebook from 2012)	1 billion	4	$7 billion	500	2010
YouTube (owned by Google from 2006)	1.3 billion	80	$4 billion	3–4,000	2005
WhatsApp (owned by Facebook from 2014)	1.5 billion	80	$5 billion	>200	2009
Twitter	300 million	12	$2.5 million	4,000	2006
Snapchat	300 million	5	$1.1 billion	1,500	2011
Spotify	207 million	36	$6 billion	4,200	2008

https://www.quora.com/
https://www.theverge.com/
https://www.digitalinformationworld.com/
http://www.businessofapps.com/
https://www.investopedia.com/.

Table 1.2 indicates that although the social media companies were established more recently, three of these companies listed in the table (Instagram, YouTube, and WhatsApp) have been acquired by the major companies in Table 1.1, thus consolidating their position.

Publications from the R&D laboratories of such major companies give a general indication of the directions they are following in some areas of their work [10–12]. However, they are unlikely to release key information which would be useful to competitors. There is also increasing concern that a small number of companies have a large amount of data about their users and are currently using it solely for their own financial benefit. Should the profits such companies make from user data be shared with the users? European regulators take strong positions on competition and privacy, and a number of the big companies have allegedly broken European anti-trust rules and have already received billion-dollar fines [13]. What may be regarded in the USA as entrepreneurialism may be seen in Europe as infringing regulations. Any fledgling company that appears likely to offer competition to one of the major companies is taken over by them, which immediately makes all its user data and intellectual property available to the parent company. The major companies have acquired an average of one company per week over recent years [13].

1.6 Research and Development in the Academy

1.6.1 National Science Foundation

The National Science Foundation (NSF) initiated a national program around data which involved the following areas:

- The foundation of data science;
- Algorithms and systems for data science;
- Data-intensive science and engineering;
- Data cyberinfrastructure; and
- Education and workforce development [14].

This reflects the multidisciplinary nature of data science. This NSF program seeks to establish a theoretical, technical, and ethical framework for data science and its impact on society.

In 2018, the NSF made available $10 million to fund 8–11 projects to harness the data revolution [15] according to a set of long-term research goals set out in 2016 [16]. This initiative, Harnessing the Data Revolution (HDR), was defined as follows:

> *The HDR vision is realized* via *a coordinated set of program solicitations resulting in an ecosystem of interrelated activities enabling (i) research in the foundations of data science; frameworks, algorithms, and systems for data science; and data-driven research in science and engineering; (ii) advanced cyberinfrastructure; and (iii) education and workforce development—all of which are designed to amplify the intrinsically multidisciplinary nature of the data science challenge. The HDR Big Idea will establish theoretical, technical, and ethical data science frameworks, and apply them to practical problems in science and engineering, and in society more generally.*

> The *Data Science Corps is one of the components of the HDR ecosystem, focusing on building capacity for harnessing the data revolution at the local, state, national, and international levels to help unleash the power of data in the service of science and society. The Data Science Corps will provide practical experiences, teach new skills, and offer teaching opportunities, in a variety of settings, to data scientists and data science students. It will also strive to promote data literacy and provide basic training in data science to the existing workforce across communities* [16].

1.6.2 European Union

The European Union (EU) has defined a number of programs for data science and big data [17] and a number of projects have been funded [18]. The H2020 ICT Work Programme 2018–19 encompasses the following areas: big data technologies and extreme-scale analytics; supporting the emergence of data markets and the data economy; and High-Performance Computing (HPC) and big data-enabled large-scale test beds and applications [18].

1.6.3   United Kingdom

In 2016, the Engineering and Physical Sciences Research Council (EPSRC) committed £10 million to fund 3–4 programs of research to

> support new approaches to data science driven by real world challenges, with projects
> undertaken in close collaboration by teams of researchers from the Mathematical Sciences
> and/or ICT, together with researchers in other disciplines and end-users [19].

In 2018, the UK Research and Innovation initiated a £48 million Artificial Intelligence (AI) and data science program to transform engineering, urban planning, and health care [20, 21]. Artificial intelligence and data is one of the four Industrial Strategy Grand Challenges outlined by the UK government [22].

The Arts and Humanities Research Council (AHRC) has also funded a number of data projects to fulfill the following general aims:

> The AHRC recognises the opportunities for transformative research in the arts and human-
> ities offered by the rapid developments in so called 'big data'. These developments include
> increased capacity to develop, exploit and re-use very large and complex datasets and novel
> methods to link together large and varied forms of data in increasingly sophisticated ways.
> We also recognise the distinctive and creative contributions that the arts and humanities can
> make to the development of approaches to the use of such 'big data'. Arts and humanities
> research is fundamental to, for example, developing new types of visualisation and represen-
> tation, exploring different contexts in which 'big data' might be used, or inspiring creative
> new ways to engage with data users.

> For researchers to meaningfully engage with information on such a large scale, it is necessary
> to develop new, or draw on innovative existing, tools and methods. With such tools, 'big data'
> can be investigated for a purpose other than the purpose it was collected for. Researchers
> can ask it different kinds of questions, use different methodologies and produce new insights.
> 'Big data' approaches can also create new cross-disciplinary and international collaborative
> research opportunities and stimulate novel boundary crossing research e.g. across different
> forms of physical and virtual materials, spanning wide geographical and temporal scales
> and combining data from different sources (research, wider publics, heritage sector, creative
> economy etc.) [23].

In 2019, the Biotechnology and Biological Sciences Research Council (BBSRC) injected £45 million for data and building infrastructure to support major advances in areas such as drug discovery, cancer genetics, regenerative medicine, and crop disease prevention over the coming decades [24].

1.7   The General Data Protection Regulation

The European General Data Protection Regulation (GDPR) [25] which came into force in May 2018 enables individuals to choose how information about them is being used. Should users be allowed to move their data to platforms whose rules on privacy they prefer, thus giving the users more control? Should competitor companies be able to request anonymized data from the big corporations in order to test out their own software in order to develop it and make it more competitive?

1.8 Conclusions

The rise in importance of data science has been driven by the increasing availability of computing resources and the avalanche of data being produced by users and instrumentation. In particular, online users generate a data trail when they access Internet functions and services. Extracting meaning from this data is one of the challenges for the major companies who deliver these services. Data science is not limited to science and engineering areas but applies equally to the biosciences, and the arts and humanities. Significant challenges arise from working with any kind of data, such as ethics, privacy, and trust, as well as questions surrounding intellectual property and copyright.

References

1. Ceruzzi, P.E.: Computing: A Concise History. MIT Press, Cambridge, MA (2012)
2. Turing, D.: The Story of Computing. Arcturus Publishing, London (2018)
3. https://en.wikipedia.org/wiki/Data_science
4. Kelleher, J.D., Tierney, B.: Data Science. MIT Press, Cambridge, MA (2018)
5. https://www.statista.com/statistics/273018/number-of-internet-users-worldwide/
6. Hamming, R.W:. Numerical Methods for Scientists and Engineers. McGraw-Hill, New York (1962, 1973)
7. Gross, M.: Introduction. In: Visual Computing. Computer Graphics: Systems and Applications. Springer, Berlin, Heidelberg (1994)
8. McCormick, B.H., De Fanti, T.A., Brown, M.D.: Visualization in scientific computing. Comput. Graph. **21**(6) (1987) (ACM SIGGRAPH). https://www.evl.uic.edu/entry.php?id=1501, https://dl.acm.org/citation.cfm?id=41997, https://www.siggraph.org//publications/video-review/1_36.php
9. Barroso, L.A., Clidaras, J., Holzle, U.: The Data Center as a Computer: An Introduction to the Design of Warehouse-Scale Machines. Morgan & Claypool, San Rafael, CA (2013)
10. Ghemawat, S., Gobloff, H., Leung, S-T.: The Google file system. ACM SIGOPS Oper. Syst. Rev. **37**(5) (2003)
11. Chang, F., Dean, J., Ghemawat, S., Hsieh, W.C., Wallach, W.A., Burrows, M., Chandra, T., Fikes, A., Gruber, R.E.: Bigtable: a distributed storage system for structured data. ACM Trans. Comput. Syst. **26**(2) (2008). https://dl.acm.org/citation.cfm?id=1365816, https://ai.google/research/pubs/pub27898
12. McKusick, M., Quinlan, S.: GFS: evolution on fast-forward. Commun. ACM **53**(3), 42–49 (2010)
13. The Determinators: Europe takes on the Tech Giants. The Economist, 23 Mar 2019
14. https://www.nsf.gov/cise/harnessingdata/
15. https://www.research.psu.edu/node/3451
16. https://www.nsf.gov/news/special_reports/big_ideas/index.jsp
17. https://ec.europa.eu/eurostat/cros/content/big-data-and-data-science_en
18. https://ec.europa.eu/digital-single-market/en/eu-funded-projects-data
19. https://epsrc.ukri.org/funding/calls/newapproachestodatascience/
20. https://www.ukri.org/news/major-new-ai-and-data-science-programme-to-transform-engineering-urban-planning-and-healthcare/
21. https://www.turing.ac.uk/news/alan-turing-institute-spearhead-new-cutting-edge-data-science-and-artificial-intelligence

22. https://www.gov.uk/government/publications/industrial-strategy-the-grand-challenges/industrial-strategy-the-grand-challenges
23. https://ahrc.ukri.org/research/fundedthemesandprogrammes/themes/digitaltransformations/bigdata/
24. https://bbsrc.ukri.org/news/research-technologies/2019/190314-n-boost-big-data-bioinformatics-research-to-drive-discovery/
25. General Data Protection Regulation (GDPR): https://eugdpr.org/

Chapter 2
Big Data

John Dill

Abstract A major business trend for most organizations is big data and business analytics, along with mobile, cloud, and social media technologies. Big data may be characterized by its volume, velocity, and variety. Most data are heterogenous and unstructured as it contains mixed and often indeterminate amounts of different kinds of information such as text, images, dates, numbers, and other information in various formats. Data analysts and scientists spend most of their time in preparing, cleaning, and wrangling their data. Data analytics may be divided into descriptive analytics, predictive analytics, and prescriptive analytics. The continuing growth of data means that large-scale analytics becomes critical for business competitiveness, and also facilitating internal decision-making processes based on data internal to the organization. Big data requires complex and advanced visualization techniques in order to fully understand the information contained in the data. Machine learning and deep learning methods are being integrated into data analytics processes. Machine learning uses statistical techniques to give computer systems the ability to "learn" (i.e., progressively improve performance on a specific task) with data. Current issues and challenges with big data and its analysis are reviewed.

Keywords Large-scale data analytics · Market size · Structure and unstructured data · MapReduce · Hadoop · Big Table · Machine learning · Descriptive analytics · Predictive analytics · Prescriptive analytics · Business intelligence · Data wrangling · Data provenance

2.1 Introduction to Big Data

2.1.1 Background

Big Data (BD) has received a great deal of attention in both the professional/technical and nontechnical literature on topics from email through blogs, social media to environmental and health analyses. An IBM survey by Gokhale [1] identified big

© The Author(s), under exclusive license to Springer Nature Switzerland AG 2019
R. Earnshaw et al., *Data Science and Visual Computing*,
SpringerBriefs in Advanced Information and Knowledge Processing,
https://doi.org/10.1007/978-3-030-24367-8_2

data and business analytics as a major business trend for most organizations, along with mobile, cloud, and social business technologies.

Application areas include the following [2]:

- *healthcare (monitoring and through integration across providers),*
- *urban planning (intelligent transportation through analysis and visualization of live and detailed road network data),*
- *environmental modeling (through sensor networks ubiquitously collecting data)*
- *energy saving (through unveiling patterns of use)*
- *smart materials (through the new materials genome initiative)*
- *machine translation between natural languages (through analysis of large corpora)*
- *education (particularly with online courses)*
- *computational social sciences (a new methodology growing fast in popularity because of the dramatically lowered cost of obtaining data)*
- *systemic risk analysis in finance (through integrated analysis of a web of contracts to find dependencies between financial entities)*
- *homeland security (through analysis of social networks and financial transactions of possible terrorists)*
- *computer security (through analysis of logged events, known as Security Information and Event Management, or SIEM), and so on [2].*

Industry and businesses have strong interests in this area, because of its applications [3]. Companies are experiencing expanding cycles of change from competition and also from applications of BD analytics which are being used as competitive weapons. A key point is:

> *the cumulative reach and scope of the underlying technologies and methods in use today reflect a level of impact on organizations that makes large-scale analytics critical for both sustaining business competitiveness and enhancing day-to-day decision making* [3].

However, it is clear that the current volume and velocity of the data are overwhelming many companies' abilities to fully cope with it. Employment opportunities in BD and data science will increase according to a McKinsey report [4]. 140,000–190,000 workers with "deep analytical" experience will be needed in the U.S.A. alone. An application in transportation [2] demonstrates that in seeking to make use of BD, a number of problems are encountered that are outside the purview of the underlying technology, and that are more "organizational" in nature.

Current trends in BD include the following [5]:

- *Data from the Internet of Things increasing dramatically: data is different from that which BD currently focusses on.*
- *Difficulties in dealing with information privacy, biases, distinguishing causation from correlation*
- *Problems with predictive models, since models built by 'inherently biased' humans (e.g. no one thought Trump would win).*
- *Potential breakthrough areas: potential for Machine Learning (ML) + Statistics via reinforcement learning, deep learning to identify structure I high-dimensional data*
- *A major unsolved problem: improving data integration, making it more seamless [5].*

2.1.2 Defining Big Data

Big data refers generally to collections of data too large to handle with "traditional" methods of a single computer-disk system. Aspects of BD include capturing data, data storage, data analysis, search, sharing, transfer, visualization, visual analytics, querying, updating, and information privacy [6]. Data and visual analysis techniques (visual analytics, information visualization, scientific visualization, and geometric visualization) are mutually dependent. When the data become "big", it must be handled using complex and advanced techniques. Correspondingly, big data requires complex and advanced visualization techniques.

According to Press [7], the first documented use of big data was in 1997 by NASA scientists [8] dealing with a visualization problem (i.e., computer graphics) which:

> *provides an interesting challenge for computer systems: data sets are generally quite large, taxing the capacities of main memory, local disk, and even remote disk. We call this the problem of big data. When data sets do not fit in main memory (in core), or when they do not fit even on local disk, the most common solution is to acquire more resources [8].*

It has been claimed that the term originated with John Mashey in 1998 at Silicon Graphics Inc. [9] when scientific visualization data to be analyzed and visualized were too large to fit in the computer's memory. Today, the term more generally refers to ultra-large collections of data, too large to be dealt with by a single processor configuration. Informally—and often inaccurately—the term has come to include almost all collections of data, whether they can be handled by a single processor or need specialized infrastructures. Some even include the infrastructure of clusters of computers and mass storage to hold and manage the data, and to the software infrastructure to create, retrieve, and analyze such large collections.

However, the generally accepted authoritative definition of big data came from Laney [10]. The three Vs—volume, velocity, and variety—have become the standard way to characterize big data. *Volume* is simply the amount of data generated and stored (Terabytes/Exabytes …, records, transactions, tables, files), *velocity* is the rate at which data are being generated (and processed if possible: batch, near time, real time, streaming), and variety is the number of different types of data (structured, unstructured, semi-structured). Often two additional terms, *veracity* and *value,* are added to more completely characterize the data. Veracity refers to the quality of the data, the degree to which data are accurate, clean, and trusted. Often thought of as accurate and reliable, real-world data are usually uncertain, messy, and contains errors.

There are a great variety of definitions according to Press [7] other than "too big for one computer." Mayer-Schonberger and Cukier [11] present a definition that points to what can be done with the data and why its size matters:

> *The ability of society to harness information in novel ways to produce useful insights or goods and services of significant value" and "…things one can do at a large scale that cannot be done at a smaller one, to extract new insights or create new forms of value [11].*

From the above, it is clear there is no single definition of "big data." For the purposes of this book, we define big data to be a collection of data, of one or more types, that is too large to handle efficiently with traditional methods running on a traditional single computer system.

2.1.3 Data Volume

But how much data makes the data large? In 2010, Eric at the Techonomy conference in Lake Tahoe in California stated that:

> there were 5 exabytes of information created by the entire world between the dawn of civilization and 2003. Now that same amount is created every two days [12].

However, Moore [13] suggested the evidence for Schmidt's statement was not strong, and that a more accurate—though less sensational—quote would have been "**23 Exabytes of information was recorded and replicated in 2002. We now record and transfer that much information every 7 days**."

Figure 2.1 shows the growth of storage capacity.

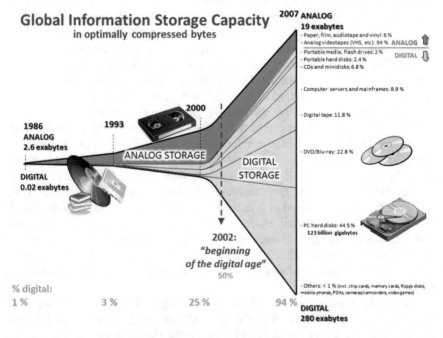

Fig. 2.1 Growth of global information storage capacity 1986 to 2007 (*Source* http://www. martinhilbert.net/WorldInfoCapacity.html). Licensed under the Creative Commons Attribution-Share Alike 3.0 Unported license. Available by licence CC BY-NC-ND 4.0. https://commons. wikimedia.org/wiki/File:Hilbert_InfoGrowth.png

Typical desktop disk drives are now upward of a Terabyte—1,000 Gb. An IBM study notes that an additional 2.5 Eb is being generated daily [14]. This amounts to 2.5 million 1-Terabyte disk drives. Additionally,

- *Over 90% of that data was generated in the last two years alone.*
- *Over 3.7 billion humans use the internet*
- *On average, Google processes over 40,000 searches a second (3.5 billion/day)*
- *Worldwide about 3.5 billion searches a day are made, most of course using Google [14].*

2.1.4 Market Size Implications

Statista [15] indicates a market size for big data in 2018 as $42 billion and rising to $56 billion in 2020 and $90 billion in 2025. Worldwide big data market revenues for software and services are projected to increase from $42B in 2018 and to $103B in 2027, attaining a Compound Annual Growth Rate (CAGR) of 10.48% according to Wikibon [16]. According to Forrester [17, 18], the big data software market will be worth $13B this year, up 14% in a year.

The rise of big data has increased the requirement for information management specialists in general, and data scientists in particular. IBM predicts that the demand for data scientists will increase by 28% to 700,000 by 2020. Data Science and Analytics (DSA) is distributed across various sectors [19]. However, skills in data science, machine learning, and big data can be the most difficult to recruit, due to the current lack of sufficiently well-qualified personnel. This in turn can cause delays in the implementation of company plans with regard to big data.

2.2 The Types of Data Organizations

2.2.1 Data Types

What does such data consist of and how is it organized? Databases are generally referred to as structured data or unstructured data, though a third type, semi-structured is increasingly useful. Structured data are organized as tables of rows and columns, where each column, sometimes called a field, has a particular data type, e.g., numeric, or a restricted text string such as a person's name, or a city name. Usually, each table will represent a single entity type, e.g., "customer". Such tables of columns and rows can easily be ordered and processed by data mining tools. Such tables are usually indexed (a requirement for relational databases) searchable by simple, straightforward search engine algorithms, and also incorporated into a relational database. Structured data omit much relevant information about a business and its operations, since such information is often in the form of text documents (Word, PDF

	Row ID	Order ID	Order Date	Product	Sales	Qty	Profit
Structured	1	CA16-156	11/8/2016	Bookcase	261.96	2	41.9
Data	2	CA16-56	11/8/2016	Chairs	731.94	3	219.6
	3	CA16-138	6/12/2016	Labels	14.62	2	6.9
	4	US15-10	10/11/2015	Table	957.58	5	-383.0

Unstructured
Data

Fig. 2.2 Structured versus unstructured data (Courtesy of John Dill)

files, email messages, multimedia data, weblogs, social media data). Additionally, images do not fit into this simple format.

In contrast, unstructured data have no internal structure. Generally, 80–90% of data are unstructured. Types of unstructured data include email messages, weblogs, multimedia data, customer service information, social media data, audio, video, digital images, word processing files, and PDF files. Such data are heterogenous as it contains mixed and often indeterminate amounts of different kinds of information such as text, images, dates, numbers, and other information in various formats. This is illustrated in Fig. 2.2.

Semi-structured data do not follow the strict rules of relational models [20] but contains tags to separate semantic elements and enforce hierarchies of records and fields within the data. In semi-structured data, entities belonging to the same class may have different attributes even though they are grouped together, and the attributes' order is not important. Examples include XML and JSON [21]. Semi-structured data are increasingly prevalent since full-text documents, and RDBMSs are not the only forms of data anymore, and different applications need a medium for exchanging information. In object-oriented databases, one often finds semi-structured data.

2.2.2 Database Types

Database types are generally Relational (RDBMS), NoSQL, or more recently NewSQL [22, 23]. RDBMSs are restricted to structured data following the relational model and rules. The data consist of a collection of *records (tuples)*, each composed of fields (informally, tables of rows and columns). Almost all use Structured Query Language (SQL) for querying and maintaining the database. Patel [21] notes that RDBMSs are generally either transaction processing systems (OLTP) or Decision Support Systems (DSSs); transactions are typically short simple queries to read or write a small number of records (e.g., order entry system).

NoSQL (Not only SQL) databases arose to be able to deal with the growing amount of unstructured data [23]. An alternative to mainstream relational DBMS, they don't use a relational data model and typically have no SQL interface. The acronym NoSQL is often understood as "Not Only SQL", implying relational systems are a proven technology but not necessarily the optimal choice for all intended uses. DB-Engines [24] indicates NoSQL systems are a heterogeneous group, with categories such as Wide Column Stores, Document Stores, Graph DBMS, RDF Stores, Native XML DBMS, Content Stores, and Search Engines. Advantages listed are higher performance, easy distribution of data on different nodes (e.g., sharding), thereby achieving scalability and fault tolerance, higher flexibility by using a schema-free data model, and simpler administration.

Analogously with RDBMS, NoSQL systems' corresponding classes are Operational—transaction-like—and Analytical—DSS-like. The latter are based on MapReduce, Hadoop, and Spark. The two types, Operational and Analytical, have different use cases and markets [22]. This is summarized in Table 2.1.

DB-Engines [24] is a knowledge base of currently over 300 database systems, which are categorized and ranked according to popularity. Categories include Relational, document store, search engine, key-value store, and others. As of September 2018, the top four were all relational. Stonebraker [25] suggests that the role of NoSQL in industry is less significant than traditional RDBMS in part because NoSQL systems do not support the ACID standard for *atomicity, consistency, isolation, and durability* of the data.

ACID and BASE refer to quality properties of databases as follows:

ACID: *Atomicity, Consistency, Isolation, Durability*: Properties of database transactions to guarantee validity even in the presence of errors, power failures.
A single logical operation on the data is called a *transaction*, e.g., transfer funds from one bank account to another.
BASE: A less demanding consistency model: Basically Available, Soft state, Eventual consistency.

Table 2.1 RDBMS and NoSQL

	RDBMS	NoSQL
Transactions	OLTP (order entry)	Operational
Analysis	DSS (sales analysis)	Analytical (based on MapReduce, Hadoop, Spark)

Fig. 2.3 Diagram of an example database according to the relational model (Courtesy of U.S. Department of Transportation vectorization: Own work—Data Integration Glossary, Public Domain, https://commons.wikimedia. org/w/index.php?curid= 17875170)

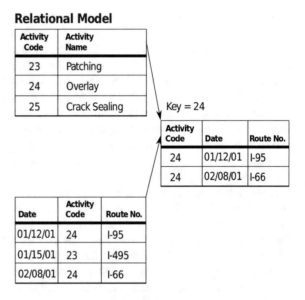

Relational Model

Activity Code	Activity Name
23	Patching
24	Overlay
25	Crack Sealing

Key = 24

Activity Code	Date	Route No.
24	01/12/01	I-95
24	02/08/01	I-66

Date	Activity Code	Route No.
01/12/01	24	I-95
01/15/01	23	I-495
02/08/01	24	I-66

2.3 Basic Big Data Architecture—How It Works

2.3.1 Relational Model

Big data systems have several components to help deal with data that may be too big for a single disk and processor. Data must be replicated since component failure must be provided for, and a distributed file system—distributed over up to hundreds or thousands of commodity processors and file servers—is normally required. It is useful to briefly consider how these systems evolved. The initial stage of Database Management Systems (DBMS) development, as data grew from simple collections and tables, was the relational model [20]. Figure 2.3 illustrates this model. This consists basically of tables of rows and columns, with rules for relating the tables in ways that maximized the effectiveness of memory and kept the data consistent via the relational rules. Such data are considered to be "structured" data. Along with RDBMS came a way of asking questions of it through SQL, a Structured Query Language. As data grew, the need for additional abstraction led to the Entity-Relationship model [26]. Relational databases continued to grow and continue to be in active use today.

2.3.2 Unstructured Data

Most data in the world are not neatly structured, or structurable, into rows and fields or columns, and the amount of such data continues to grow. Fortunately, the cost of computing and storage continues to decrease, to a level where very powerful systems are at the "commodity" level, and clusters of computers and storage are (relatively) inexpensive. But what is needed is a way of managing the clusters and supporting access to them. More importantly, analysis (data analytics) of such data is required. The related development of high-performance, high-reliability, and low-cost Internet access meant that such clusters could be remote from a user—i.e., in the "cloud". Therefore, BD is not a single technology; it is the capability to manage huge volumes of disparate data, and allow appropriate access to support a variety of analysis methods—data analytics. Analysis of big data is of course iterative, cycling from data capture through organizing the data, integrating it with existing data, applying analysis algorithms and making decisions based on the analysis, and continuing back to more data capture.

2.3.3   MapReduce, Hadoop, and Big Table

Three technologies arose out of the requirement of Google, Yahoo, and Facebook to deal with the massive amounts of data inherent in their services. These are MapReduce, Hadoop, and Big Table. MapReduce was developed by Google to execute a function against a large amount of distributed data in batch mode. "Map" distributes the tasks across the nodes in a cluster so as to load balance and deal with component failure, while "Reduce", after the task completes, gathers the elements back together into a result.

Hadoop is open-source software which provides a framework for using the MapReduce model on a network of computers, whether low cost or high end. It provides redundancy to enable hardware failures to be handled automatically. It consists of a distributed file system and processing components. Data are distributed across network nodes and then processed in parallel. It is therefore able to utilize data locality where processing concentrates on each node.

Traditional RDBMSs, though effective, are difficult to scale with increasing data. One of the purposes of Google's Big Table (BT) was to allow structured relational databases to grow, and is a sparse, distributed persistent multidimensional sorted map. BT is intended to store huge volumes of data across commodity servers. BT was also designed to support unstructured data.

2.3.4   Components of Big Data Architectures

Big data architecture must handle ingestion, processing, and transforming data into file systems or database structures, and also protect against equipment and power failures. It must support a suitable "data server" mechanism with support for sufficient volume, and be able to expand as volume and variety increase, ideally run on commodity hardware, and also allow for data replication for increased reliability.

Microsoft [27] notes that a BD system usually involves some combination of batch processing of static data, real-time processing of dynamic/streaming data, interactive exploration of big data and predictive analytics, and machine learning. Therefore, it has to be able to support a variety of analytics tools, and analyst queries run in the environment, to extract information and intelligence from data, which outputs to a variety of different vehicles.

Big data architectures are typically built on large-scale distributed clusters with scalable performance and capacity. System health is monitored via central management consoles. A basic choice is to install a local system or use the Cloud/Cloud service for which capital costs are lower, but planning and monitoring are still required. The architectural components include the following [28]:

- *Data sources layer: data from a variety of sources including social media, email, IoT, other data warehouses.*

- *Data massage/storage layer: ingest data from sources. Convert to appropriate format; may use RTDBMS for structured data, specialized file systems like Hadoop Distributed File System (HDFS) or a NoSQL database.*

- *Analysis layer: multiple analytics tools, sampling related tools for structured data, ML and advanced tools for unstructured data*

- *Consumption layer: present analysis results to human viewers, applications and business processes [28].*

Major steps in the analysis of big data are shown in the flow of the Big Data pipeline [29].

2.4 Data Analytics

2.4.1 The Objective of Data Analytics

Gartner [30] states that advanced analytics is the autonomous or semi-autonomous examination of data or content using sophisticated techniques and tools. Typically, these are beyond those of traditional Business Intelligence (BI) and are used to discover deeper insights, make predictions, or generate recommendations. Advanced analytic techniques include those such as statistical modeling, data/text mining, machine learning, pattern matching, forecasting, visualization, semantic analysis, sentiment analysis, network and cluster analysis, multivariate statistics, graph analysis, simulation, complex event processing, and neural networks. For most organizations, the goal of big data initiatives is to generate insights the organization can use to become more efficient, better serve customers, or become more competitive.

2.4.2   Tools for Data Analytics

Big data analytics tools to accomplish this include data mining, business intelligence, predictive analytics, machine learning, cognitive computing, artificial intelligence, search, and data modeling solutions. An overview is provided by Tavi and Krishna [31].

Analytics tools can be thought of as descriptive, predictive, or prescriptive, as follows:

Descriptive   gather, organize, describe; dashboards; "reporting"; "What has happened?"; no information on why it happened.

Predictive   use existing data to model or predict future, e.g., a given customer type will respond better to a particular type of advertisement/image. "What could happen?"

Prescriptive   advise on a course of action; cause and effect analysis. "What should we do?"

Predictive analytics has a long history arising out of statistics and statistical predictions and is common in many business applications. It is therefore not necessarily reliant on current techniques used in machine learning and data mining. The characteristics of analytics tools can be combined in different ways and then applied to the domain problems (e.g., business). Press [7] notes the growing maturity of the BD concept and shows the difference between big data and Business Intelligence (BI) as follows:

- BI uses **descriptive statistics** on high-density datasets to measure things, detect trends, etc.
- BD uses **inductive statistics** on low-density large datasets to infer laws, find relationships, and predict outcomes.

The differences between these domains may be summarized as follows:

Business intelligence: a process for analyzing data and presenting actionable information to help executives;
Business analytics: exploration of a firm's data, emphasizing statistical analysis; for data-driven decision-making;
Big data analytics: examining large datasets to uncover hidden patterns to make better decisions.

2.4.3   Machine Learning

The use of Machine Learning (ML) and so-called deep learning methods are growing rapidly. ML uses statistical techniques to give computer systems the ability to "learn" (i.e., progressively improve performance on a specific task) with data, without being explicitly programmed to do so. ML algorithms learn from and make predictions on, data through building a model from sample inputs. Example applications include email filtering, detection of network intruders, and computer vision. ML is related to (and often overlaps with) computational statistics, which also focuses on prediction-making through the use of computers. ML is sometimes conflated with data mining, which focuses more on exploratory data analysis and is known as unsupervised learning.

In data analytics, ML is used to devise complex models and algorithms that lend themselves to prediction. In commercial use, this is known as *predictive analytics*. These analytical models allow analysts to "*produce reliable, repeatable decisions and results*" and uncover "*hidden insights*" through learning from historical relationships and trends in the data [32]. R2D3 [33] provides a dynamic visual example of machine learning.

Many ML applications and Neural Nets operate as a "black boxes"—they will arrive at an "answer" but provide no hint as to how or why that answer was arrived at [34]. As an example, a program "Deep Patient" was particularly good at predicting which patients were likely to become schizophrenic, a difficult task for physicians, but the program could provide no information on how it arrived at its recommendations. The problem is currently being addressed by an Artificial Intelligence (AI) system for mining pathology which reports snippets of text that represent a pattern discovered by the network [34].

Microsoft [35] summarizes the main categories of training as supervised and unsupervised learning as follows:

> **Supervised** is more common. The data scientist teaches the algorithm conclusions it should come up with; this requires outputs already known and data used to train algorithm already labeled with correct answers. For example, a classification algorithm learns to identify animals after being trained on a dataset of images properly labeled with species and some identifying characteristics. The goal is to specify the function well enough so that when new input data is given, it can predict output.

> **Unsupervised** machine learning is closer to true AI—the computer "learns" to identify complex processes and patterns without human guidance. Although unsupervised learning is prohibitively complex for some simpler enterprise use cases, it opens the doors to solving problems that humans normally would not normally attempt. Some examples of unsupervised machine learning algorithms include k-means clustering, principal and independent component analysis, and association rules. The goal is to model hidden patterns of underlying structure in given input data in order to learn about the data.

> **Deep Learning:** techniques based on the use of mathematical 'neural nets' that simulate a collection of interconnected neurons [35].

2.5   Business Intelligence

Business intelligence is aggregated information obtained from inside a company which can provide a quantitative picture of its overall performance (e.g., the cost of its products and services, production times, current orders, delivery times, etc.). This needs to be evaluated in the context of the external market in which the company is operating, and also the competing businesses. Is the company holding its own, or gaining, or losing, market share? The external market can be a complex set of information, but without it the company cannot understand how it is performing relative to other businesses, and how to optimally position itself to maximize its impact on the market. When the internal data are combined with the external data, it can be considered as "intelligent" data which provides a view of the overall situation of the company.

In general, detailed internal information is available to a business to evaluate its performance such as financial statements, marketing statements, product evaluations, and staffing reports. Often these can be summarized in key performance indicators and displayed on a dashboard. Analysis of the external information can identify market trends and, by implication, any changes that may be necessary in order for the business to maintain, or increase, its market share. Forrester Research defines business intelligence as "*a set of methodologies, processes, architectures, and technologies that transform raw data into meaningful and useful information used to enable more effective strategic, tactical, and operational insights and decision-making*" [36]. Business intelligence may use visual display tools similar to those used in the context of big data. However, the latter is normally concerned with much more complex data where the information density may be low, and where the relationships between parts of the data may be unclear or unknown. Business data analysis is usually based on regular data and this is normally reported to senior management for them to make any decisions that may be necessary for the effective operation and direction of the company on a day-to-day basis.

A Gartner magic quadrant gives a view of the market's competitors in terms of the characteristics of leaders, challengers, niche players, or visionaries [37].

2.6 The Use and Impact of Big Data

Obama Political Campaign

At the time of the Presidential Election in the USA in 2012, quantitative analyst and New York Times blogger, Nate Silver, specified the results accurately in every single state by using analytical methods [38–40]. The Obama campaign analyzed large amounts of data on voter behavior and then used a variety of digital methods to influence voters including the following:

- Metric-driven email campaigns,
- Quick Donate program gave almost four times more than from other donation methods,
- Analyzing voters' movements in key states,
- Advertisements placed in social media,

- Q&A session held on Reddit because the data showed that target voters used Reddit,
- Emails to voters from Obama's wife had a better effect then from other people, and
- Analyzing economic variables.

Thus, the Obama political campaign was driven by analyzing social media data for useful and strategic information which it could exploit to sway voters, particularly in marginal states. Ceron [41] details some of the problems with social media data and how sentiment analysis can yield more accurate analyses for prediction purposes. Johnson [42] looks at the digital techniques of modern political campaigning such as micro-targeting, online fundraising, digital communication, and the use of new media.

2.7 Current Trends in Big Data

Businesses are moving to be data-driven enterprises [43]. Heller [44] regards big data, machine learning, and data science as key areas, and they are expanding rapidly. Lebied [45] highlights AI and predictive and prescriptive analytics tools. Carillo [46] notes the growth in IoT networks and the development of accessible AI. In summary, some overall common themes are as follows: increased use of predictive analytics, (deep) neural nets, more focus on data governance and data quality (wrangling methodologies), IoT growth, and AI.

2.8 Current Issues and Challenges

2.8.1 A Problem of Perception

Much of the "blogosphere" refers to all data, whether large or small, as "Big Data", and while many analysis approaches can apply to any size of data, working with big data is different in a number of ways [47]. A "spreadsheet size" file fits in memory can be cleaned relatively easily and processed quickly. Big data does not fit in memory and cannot be handled and processed in such a straightforward way. Computations are usually done in batches and can take a long time. Data are kept on clusters of processing/storage nodes. Data cannot be simply copied to a disk, and an analysis run "in real time." As Fisher et al. [47] note, *"the luxuries of interactivity, direct manipulation, and fast system response are gone"*; methods are similar to the historic environments of batch runs and punched cards: data are prepared, the job is submitted, and the results are collected some time later. Fisher et al. [47] interviewed analysts whose tasks varied from twitter feed analysis to ML analysis of search queries. The common work pattern was as follows: acquire data, choose an architecture, shape the data to the architecture, write/edit/debug code, and then iterate on the results.

This workflow—Cloud computation—is vastly different from local computing, whether Amazon Elastic Compute Cloud (EC2), Hadoop cluster, or Microsoft Azure. Debugging is inconvenient, time-consuming, and frustrating. Interestingly, many analysts stressed the importance of visualization to inspect data at multiple scales.

2.8.2 Sampling

Analysis of data collections and populations has traditionally relied on sampling—building models based on data from a small *sample* of a larger population. Big data adds both solutions and problems. Fan et al. [48] note

> many traditional methods that perform well for moderate sample size do not scale to massive data. Similarly, many statistical methods that perform well for low-dimensional data are facing significant challenges in analyzing high-dimensional data [48].

It is sometimes claimed that with big data that there is no longer any need to be concerned about sampling; "all" the data can be used. Naimi et al. [49] note that this isn't always valid. "All" the data aren't always available, even to big data. For example, information from an analysis of tweets almost invariably overlooks the fact that use of Twitter by American adults decreases by age—from 27% (30–49 years) to 8% (over 65 years) [50]. And the bias of "more is always better" leads to claiming a larger messier dataset is preferable to a smaller less messy dataset. This is, however, a difficult, nonobvious issue—e.g., in epidemiology.

2.8.3 Data Cleaning and Wrangling

This may be one of the more important areas due to the critical need and, until recently, neglect by the community, leading to a scarcity of tools. Even today blogs and analyses indicate that industry data analysts and scientists spend most of their time in preparing, cleaning and wrangling their data—before any analysis, and there appears to be only a modest amount of significant research in this area.

Gartner [51] notes that data analytics teams spend more time wrangling data than building insights. It suggests, even with all the hype about performance and ML and analytics, that basic problems such as data cleaning/wrangling are still largely unsolved. Stonebraker [52] notes that a recent Ph.D. in ML now working in industry said he spent 90% of his time finding the right data. Even having found suitable data, it can be difficult getting permission to access it [53].

Wrangling is transforming and mapping data from one raw data form into another format with the intent of making it more appropriate and valuable for a variety of downstream purposes such as analytics. Tools include Excel, SQL, and Trifacta

Wrangler. Green [54] adds the following: Tabula for PDF to Spreadsheet, OpenRe-fine—open-source, programmable expressions, R packages, DataWrangler, CSVKit (converts among Excel, CSV, JSON, Query, SQL), Mr. Data Converter (Excel to HTML/JSON/XML).

The types of skills needed, and the challenges faced by real-world analysts in trying to format/wrangle data, are significant [55].

Chu et al. [56] note:

> data quality remains to be a major concern, and dirty data can lead to incorrect decisions and unreliable analysis. Examples of common errors include missing values, typos, mixed formats, replicated entries of the same real-world entity, and violations of business rules [56].

Cleaning the data is a critical precursor to developing any analytic method. This includes detecting missing data, dealing with improbable values and duplications, correcting data entry problems, and rectifying faulty sensors. This is almost always more complex, difficult, and time-consuming than analysts expect [57]. Gupta and Rani [58] state that poor data quality has become a serious problem, noting it is "*a tedious task and it consumes around 30%-80% of the development time and budget.*"

2.8.4 Provenance

Data provenance is information about the origin and creation process of data. Such information is useful for debugging data and transformations, auditing, evaluating the quality of and trust in data, modeling authenticity, and implementing access control for derived data. Provenance has been studied by the database, workflow, and distributed systems communities, but provenance for big data is a largely unexplored field [59]. Wang et al. [60] consider big data provenance relative to data veracity and the provenance of the analytical processes. Challenges include the large size of the provenance data itself, provenance collection overhead, dealing with distributed provenance, and reproducing an execution from big data provenance data. It is also relevant to understand more than just the origin of the data, but also the origin of the information derived from the data through analysis [61].

2.8.5 General Issues

Marr [62] suggests 50% of big data projects will fail to deliver against expectations, with most of the reasons being management-related such as lack of clear objectives, poor business case, etc. rather than issues to do with technology.

Kugler [63] notes Google's influenza forecasting service which used BD failed to predict the 2013 flu outbreak. Similarly, an effort to predict Ebola's spread in 2014 gave inaccurate results. The causes were failing to partner with traditional data collection and analysis ("big data hubris") and algorithm dynamics—Google's search algorithms changed many times over while developers were working on the flu algorithm.

Many research challenges arise in the context of data heterogeneity, inconsistency and incompleteness, timeliness, privacy, visualization, and collaboration, to the tools ecosystem around big data:

> *Research Challenges abound, ranging from heterogeneity of data, inconsistency and incompleteness, timeliness, privacy, visualization, and collaboration, to the tools ecosystem around Big Data* [2]

[2]. Wrangling algorithms expect homogeneous data—so data must be carefully structured prior to analysis. Real data increasingly include data from diverse sources of varying reliability and accuracy. Sometimes, the large volume can help recovery, but extensive cross-checking is required to validate the data.

In addition, the most difficult problems are never "one time through"; difficult problems always require iteration—with a human making critical decisions, based on interacting with visualizations of the data. Visual analytics directly addresses this issue but is only recently being recognized within the BD field:

> *In spite of the tremendous advances made in computational analysis, there remain many patterns that humans can easily detect but computer algorithms have a difficult time finding. For example, CAPTCHAs exploit precisely this fact to tell human Web users apart from computer programs. Ideally, analytics for Big Data will not be all computational— rather it will be designed explicitly to have a human in the loop. The new subfield of visual analytics is attempting to do this, at least with respect to the modeling and analysis phase in the pipeline* [64].

The need for human-in-the-loop approaches was also emphasized by Ebert [65]—focusing on how visual analytics can improve the decision-making process in business:

> *To solve the world's challenges requires not only advancing computer science and big data analytics but requires new analysis and decision-making environments that effectively couple human decision-making with advanced, guided analytics in a human-computer collaborative discourse and decision-making (HCCD). Our HCCD approach builds upon visual analytics and focuses on empowering the decision maker through interactive visual analytic environments where non-digital human expertise and experience can be combined with state-of-the-art analytical techniques* [65].

2.9 Conclusions

This chapter has reviewed key aspects of big data and their relationship to the environments within which such data are generated, processed, and then analyzed. It is a complex and rapidly evolving field, simply because the gains can be significant for businesses that are able to secure a competitive edge by being able to extract key information and knowledge from their data. In addition, scientific and industrial research is under continual pressure to improve its hardware, software, strategy, and expertise in order to be able to cope with the continually increasing amounts of data of all kinds including real time, being generated.

Further Reading

Henke, N. Bughin, J. Chui, M. Manyika, J. Saleh, T. Wiseman, B, Sethupathy, G. The Age of Analytics: Competing in a Data Driven World, McKinsey Global Institute (2016). Online at—https://www.mckinsey.com/~/media/McKinsey/Business%20Functions/McKinsey%20Analytics/Our%20Insights/The%20age%20of%20analytics%20Competing%20in%20a%20data%20driven%20world/MGI-The-Age-of-Analytics-Full-report.ashx

Khalifa, S. Elshater, Y. Sundaravarathan, K. Bhat, A. Martin, P. Imam, F. Rope, D. McRoberts, M. Statchuk, C. The Six Pillars for Building Big Data Analytics Ecosystems, ACM Computing Surveys, Vol. 49, No. 2, Article 33 (2016). https://dl.acm.org/citation.cfm?id=2963143

Cao, L. Data Science: A Comprehensive Overview. ACM Computing Surveys, Vol 50 Issue 3, (2017). Online at—http://203.170.84.89/~idawis33/DataScienceLab/publication/CSUR-Datascience-overview-published.pdf

NIST. Big Data Program. Big Data Interoperability Framework (2018). Online at—https://bigdatawg.nist.gov/V2_output_docs.php

Pouyanfar, S. Yang, Y. Chen, S.C. Shyu, M.L. S. S. Iyengar, S.S. Multimedia Big Data Analytics: A Survey. ACM Computing Surveys, Vol 51 Issue 1 (2018). Online at—https://www.researchgate.net/publication/322373798_Multimedia_Big_Data_Analytics_A_Survey

Siow, E. Tiropanis, T. Hall, W. Analytics for the Internet of Things: A Survey ACM Computing Surveys, Vol 51 Issue 4 (2018). Online at—https://arxiv.org/pdf/1807.00971.pdf

Tang, J. Cui, Y. Li, Q. Ren, K. Liu, J. Buyya, R. Ensuring Security and Privacy Preservation for Cloud Data Services. ACM Computing Surveys, Vol 49, Issue 1 (2016). Online at—http://buyya.com/papers/Security-PrivacyPerservation2016.pdf

Xia, F. Wang, W. Bekele, T.M. Liu, H. Big Scholarly Data: A Survey. IEEE Transactions on Big Data. Vol 3, Issue 1 (2017). https://ieeexplore.ieee.org/document/7809016

ZDNet-Tech Republic. Sensor'd Enterprise: IoT, ML and big data. White paper (2018). Online at—https://www.techrepublic.com/resource-library/whitepapers/special-report-iot-and-the-sensor-d-enterprise-free-pdf/

Gudivada, V. N. Baeza-Yates, R. Raghavan, V. V. Big Data: Promises and Problems, Guest Editors' Introduction, IEEE Computer, Vol. 48, Issue No. 3, pp. 20–23 (2015). https://ieeexplore.ieee.org/document/7063181

Ramakrishnan N. and Kumar, R. Big Data. Guest Editors' Introduction. Special issue of IEEE Computer on Big Data. Vol. 49, No. 4, pp 21–22 (2016). Online at—https://ieeexplore.ieee.org/stamp/stamp.jsp?tp=&arnumber=7452319

References

1. Gokhale, V.: The 2011 IBM Tech Trends Report: The Clouds Are Rolling In … Is Your Business Ready? IBM, New York, NY (2011). http://ibm.co/1PlcOVR
2. Jagadish, H.V., Gehrke, J., Labrinidis, A., Papakonstantinou, Y., Patel, J.M., Ramakrishnan, R., Shahabi, C.: Big data and its technical challenges. Commun. ACM **57**(7), 86–94 (2014). https://pdfs.semanticscholar.org/e527/d3c3d02f3493097be0d0f190bdc322c7519b.pdf
3. Davis, C.K.: Communications of the ACM Viewpoint: Beyond Data and Analysis **57**(6), 39–41 (2014). https://cacm.acm.org/magazines/2014/6/175178-beyond-data-and-analysis/abstract
4. Manyika, J., Chui, M., Brown, B., Bughin, J., Dobbs, R., Roxburgh, C., Byers, A.H.: Big data: The next frontier for innovation, competition, and productivity. McKinsey Global Institute (2011). https://www.mckinsey.com/business-functions/digital-mckinsey/our-insights/big-data-the-next-frontier-for-innovation
5. Commun. ACM. Big Data **60**(6), 24–25 (2017). https://cacm.acm.org/magazines/2017/6/217731-big-data/abstract
6. https://en.wikipedia.org/wiki/Big_data
7. Press, G.: 12 Big Data Definitions: What's Yours? Forbes, 3 Sept 2014. https://www.forbes.com/sites/gilpress/2014/09/03/12-big-data-definitions-whats-yours/#2f31991613ae
8. Cox, M., Ellsworth, D.: Application-controlled demand paging for out-of-core visualization. In: Proceedings of the 8th Conference on Visualization (1997). http://dl.acm.org/citation.cfm?id=266989.267068&coll=DL&dl=GUIDE
9. Lohr, S.: The Origins of 'Big Data': An Etymological Detective Story, New York Times, 1 Feb 2013. https://bits.blogs.nytimes.com/2013/02/01/the-origins-of-big-data-an-etymological-detective-story/
10. Laney, D.: 3D Data Management: Controlling Data Volume, Velocity, and Variety. Application Delivery Strategies, META Group (2001). https://blogs.gartner.com/doug-laney/files/2012/01/ad949-3D-Data-Management-Controlling-Data-Volume-Velocity-and-Variety.pdf
11. Mayer-Schonberger, V., Cukier, K.: Big Data: A Revolution That Will Transform How We Live, Work and Think. John Murray, London, UK (2013)
12. Datafloq: A Short History of Big Data. https://datafloq.com/read/big-data-history/239
13. Moore, R.J.: https://blog.rjmetrics.com/2011/02/07/eric-schmidts-5-exabytes-quote-is-a-load-of-crap/ (2011)
14. IBM Marketing Cloud: 10 Key Marketing Trends for 2107. White Paper. https://www-01.ibm.com/common/ssi/cgi-bin/ssialias?htmlfid=WRL12345USEN, https://public.dhe.ibm.com/common/ssi/ecm/wr/en/wrl12345usen/watson-customer-engagement-watson-marketing-wr-other-papers-and-reports-wrl12345usen-20170719.pdf
15. Statista: https://www.statista.com/statistics/254266/global-big-data-market-forecast/ (2018)
16. http://wikibon.org/
17. Columbus, L.: 10 Charts That Will Change Your Perspective Of Big Data's Growth. https://www.forbes.com/sites/louiscolumbus/2018/05/23/10-charts-that-will-change-your-perspective-of-big-datas-growth/#749ec39b2926 (2018)
18. Columbus, L.: IBM Predicts Demand For Data Scientists Will Soar 28% By 2020. https://www.forbes.com/sites/louiscolumbus/2017/05/13/ibm-predicts-demand-for-data-scientists-will-soar-28-by-2020/#353567997e3b (2018)
19. https://blogs-images.forbes.com/louiscolumbus/files/2017/05/Data-Science-and-Analytics-Demand-by-industry.jpg
20. Codd, E.F.: A relational model of data for large shared data banks. Commun. ACM **13**(6), 377–387 (1970). https://doi.org/10.1145/362384.362685. https://cs.uwaterloo.ca/~david/cs848s14/codd-relational.pdf
21. https://en.wikipedia.org/wiki/Semi-structured_data
22. Patel, J.M.: Operational NoSQL systems: what's new and what's next? IEEE Comput. **49**(4), 23–30 (2016). https://www.computer.org/csdl/mags/co/2016/04/mco2016040023.html

23. Gudivada, V.N., Rao, D., Raghaven, V.V.: Renaissance in database management: navigating the landscape of candidate systems. IEEE Comput. **49**(4), 31–42 (2016). https://ieeexplore.ieee.org/document/7452311
24. DB-Engines Ranking: https://db-engines.com/en/ranking. Accessed 18 Sept 2018
25. Stonebraker, M.: Stonebraker on NoSQL and enterprises. Commun. ACM **54**(8), 10–11 (2011). https://cacm.acm.org/magazines/2011/8/114950-stonebraker-on-nosql-and-enterprises/abstract
26. https://en.wikipedia.org/wiki/Entity%E2%80%93relationship_model
27. Microsoft: Big Data Architectures (2017). https://docs.microsoft.com/en-us/azure/architecture/data-guide/big-data/
28. Taylor, C.: Big Data Architecture, Datamation, 8 June 2017 https://www.datamation.com/big-data/big-data-architecture.html
29. https://cra.org/ccc/wp-content/uploads/sites/2/2015/05/bigdatawhitepaper.pdf
30. Gartner Summits: Advanced Analytics (2018). https://www.gartner.com/it-glossary/advanced-analytics/
31. Tayi, G.M., Krishna, P.R.: IEEE Computing Now special issue on Advanced Data Analytics, Guest Editors' Introduction, Oct 2017. https://www.computer.org/publications/tech-news/computing-now/advanced-data-analytics
32. Machine Learning, Wikipedia: https://en.wikipedia.org/wiki/Machine_learning
33. R2D3: A Visual Introduction to Machine Learning. http://www.r2d3.us/visual-intro-to-machine-learning-part-1/
34. Knight, W.: The Dark Secret at the Heart of AI, MIT Technology Review, May/June 2017. https://www.technologyreview.com/s/604087/the-dark-secret-at-the-heart-of-ai/
35. Microsoft: https://docs.microsoft.com/en-us/azure/architecture/data-guide/scenarios/advanced-analytics (2017)
36. Evelson, B.: Topic Overview: Business Intelligence, 21 Nov 2008. https://www.forrester.com/report/Topic+Overview+Business+Intelligence/-/E-RES39218
37. https://en.wikipedia.org/wiki/Magic_Quadrant
38. Vijayan, J.: Presidential election a victory for quants, Computerworld (2012). https://www.computerworld.com/article/2492918/business-intelligence/presidential-election-a-victory-for-quants.html
39. Lampitt, A.: The real story of how big data analytics helped Obama win, Infoworld (2013). https://www.infoworld.com/article/2613587/big-data/the-real-story-of-how-big-data-analytics-helped-obama-win.html
40. Yan, Z.: How data analytics helped Obama win the 2012 US presidential election (2018). https://yp.scmp.com/tertiary-education/city-university-of-hong-kong/article/109120/how-data-analytics-helped-obama-win
41. Ceron, A., Curini, L., Iacus, S.M.: Politics and Big Data: Nowcasting and Forecasting Elections with Social Media. Routledge, Abingdon, UK (2017)
42. Johnson, D.W.: Campaigning in the Twenty-First Century: Activism, Big Data, and Dark Money. Routledge, Abingdon, UK (2016)
43. Olavsrud, T.: 6 data analytics trends that will dominate 2018. CIO (2018). https://www.cio.com/article/3251720/analytics/4-data-analytics-trends-that-will-dominate-2018.html
44. Heller, M.: 10 hot data analytics trends—and 5 going cold. CIO (2017). https://www.cio.com/article/3213189/analytics/10-hot-data-analytics-trends-and-5-going-cold.html
45. Lebied, M.: Top 10 Analytics And Business Intelligence Trends for 2018. Datapine (2017). https://www.datapine.com/blog/business-intelligence-trends/
46. Carillo, D.: 10 Big Data Trends you should know. Pure B2B, 2018. KDNuggets. https://www.kdnuggets.com/2018/09/10-big-data-trends.html
47. Fisher, D., Deline, R., Czerwinski, M., Drucker, S.: Interactions with big data analytics. ACM Interact. **19**(3), 50–59 (2012). https://dl.acm.org/citation.cfm?id=2168943
48. Fan, J., Fang, H., Liu, H.: Challenges of big data analysis. Natl. Sci. Rev. **1**(2), 293–314 (2014). https://doi.org/10.1093/nsr/nwt032, https://academic.oup.com/nsr/article/1/2/293/1397586

49. Naimi, A.I., Westreich, D.J.: Book Review of Big Data: A Revolution That Will Transform How We Live, Work, and Think. Am. J. Epidemiol. **179**(9), 1143–1144 (2014). https://doi.org/10.1093/aje/kwu085
50. https://blog.hootsuite.com/twitter-demographics/
51. Gartner: Gartner Marketing Analytics Survey (2018). https://www.gartner.com/smarterwithgartner/key-findings-from-gartner-marketing-analytics-survey-2018/
52. Stonebraker, M.: My 10 fears about the Future of the DBMS field (2018). https://www.youtube.com/watch?v=DJFKl_5JTnA
53. Kasik, D., Dill, J.: Toward technology transfer evaluation criteria. In: Proceedings of Hawaii International Conference on System Sciences (HICSS) (2019)
54. Green, A.: Seven Free Data Wrangling Tools (2015). https://blog.varonis.com/free-data-wrangling-tools/
55. Kandel, S., Paepcke, A., Hellerstein, J.M., Heer, J.: Enterprise data analysis and visualization: an interview study. IEEE Trans. Vis. Comput. Graph. **18**(12), 2917–2926 (2012). http://vis.stanford.edu/files/2012-EnterpriseAnalysisInterviews-VAST.pdf, https://ieeexplore.ieee.org/document/6327298
56. Chu, X., Ilyas, I.F., Krishnan, S., Wang. J.: Data cleaning: overview and emerging challenges. In: SIGMOD'16, 26 June–01 July 2016. http://dx.doi.org/10.1145/2882903.2912574. https://dl.acm.org/citation.cfm?doid=2882903.2912574
57. Shneiderman, B., Plaisant, C.: Sharpening analytic focus to cope with big data volume and variety. Visualization viewpoints. IEEE Comput. Graph. Appl. **35**(3), 10–14 (2015). https://ieeexplore.ieee.org/document/7111924, http://www.cs.umd.edu/hcil/trs/2014-27/2014-27.pdf
58. Gupta, D., Rani, R.: A study of big data evolution and research challenges. J. Inf. Sci. 1–19 (2018). https://doi.org/10.1177/0165551518789880
59. Glavic, B.: Big Data provenance: challenges and implications for benchmarking. In: Workshop on Specifying Big Data Benchmarks, vol. 8163, pp. 72–80, Springer, Cham, Switzerland (2012)
60. Wang, J., Crawl, D., Purawat, S., Nguyen, M., Altintas, I.: Big data provenance: challenges, state of the art and opportunities. In: IEEE International Conference on Big Data 2015, pp. 2509–2516 (2015). https://ieeexplore.ieee.org/document/7364047, https://www.researchgate.net/publication/301451405_Big_Data_Provenance_Challenges_State_of_the_Art_and_Opportunities
61. Ragan, E.D., Endert, A., Sanyal, J., Chen, J.: Characterizing provenance in visualization and data analysis: an organizational framework of provenance types and purposes. IEEE Trans. Vis. Comput. Graph. **22**(1), 31–40 (2016). https://ieeexplore.ieee.org/document/7192714
62. Marr, B.: Where Big Data Projects Fail, Forbes (2015). https://www.forbes.com/sites/bernardmarr/2015/03/17/where-big-data-projects-fail/#12b6463c239f
63. Kugler, L.: What happens when big data blunders? Commun. ACM **59**(6), 15–16 (2016). https://dl.acm.org/citation.cfm?id=2911975, https://cacm.acm.org/magazines/2016/6/202655-what-happens-when-big-data-blunders/abstract
64. Manoj, K.S., Dileep, K.G. (eds.): Effective Big Data Management and Opportunities for Implementation. IGI Publishing, Hershey, PA (2016). https://dl.acm.org/citation.cfm?id=3044790, http://eprints.bournemouth.ac.uk/23576/9/karanasiou%20chap_kumar%202016%20book.pdf
65. Ebert, D.: Keynote talk at the 5th annual 2017 Big Data Congress, Halifax, NS: Human-Computer Collaborative Decision Making, Through Visual Analytics, Nov 2017. https://www.conf.purdue.edu/landing_pages/psps/profile8.aspx

Chapter 3
Visual Computing

Rae Earnshaw

Abstract Visual computing regards the computer as a visual processing machine. It takes images and all forms of data and inputs them to the computer. Visual computing uses predefined algorithms to produce results in a visual form such as images, tables, or animations. The internal algorithms perform the functions that the user requires on the data. The results that are output are intended to be assimilated by a human. The input and processing phases may be subject to intervention by the user, if exploration of the input data, or steering the processing, is required. This human–computer interaction can take various forms from simple menu-driven controls to advanced virtual reality systems.

Keywords Image processing · Computer vision · Computer graphics · Visualization

3.1 Introduction

Visual computing encompasses a number of areas including visual image processing, computer graphics, visualization, computer vision, and virtual and augmented reality. It deals with creating and analyzing images. It also relies on a variety of tools and processes from other areas including human–computer interaction and pattern recognition. The mission of science and engineering is often to locate such key information using visual means. Scientific experiments are frequently designed to locate a particular effect in the physical world. Sensors are involved in monitoring environments to log events that provide more information on what is being observed. In both these instances, the computer analysis needs to be efficient, effective, reliable, and reproducible. If there are anomalies in the data, the analysis needs to be able to recognize these and decide whether they are significant or not. Similarly, business data processing is seeking to obtain more accurate information on its internal performance of the business, and also to more effectively identify external trends, markets, and customers. In an increasingly competitive global market place for products and

© The Author(s), under exclusive license to Springer Nature Switzerland AG 2019   33
R. Earnshaw et al., *Data Science and Visual Computing*,
SpringerBriefs in Advanced Information and Knowledge Processing,
https://doi.org/10.1007/978-3-030-24367-8_3

services, companies need to be able to obtain a clear and accurate picture of their position from the data that they own. Currently, there is increasing interest in using machine learning and artificial intelligence techniques to assist in the overall process of extracting information and knowledge from datasets. Such datasets are becoming increasingly large, so key information can be increasingly difficult to find. Therefore, automated or semi-automated tools are being developed and used to assist in this process.

3.2   Visual Computing in Practice

Components of visual computing include the following:

(1)   Computer graphics facilities for producing appropriate images from data;
(2)   Image analysis to extract and refine information from images;
(3)   Visualization and visual analytics to highlight key information in the results, and to select, group, and organize various levels of data;
(4)   Geometric modeling to represent objects;
(5)   Virtual and augmented reality to enable users to explore the environment of the data model; and
(6)   Human–computer interaction techniques to facilitate ergonomic interaction with the computer.

A variety of hardware and software environments are available for processing and analyzing visual and alphanumeric data. The difficulty is often integrating them into an appropriate system and providing interfaces for both trained and untrained users. Data sizes can be large and heterogenous, with different types of data at different times.

The visual computing field may be defined in large measure by what particular departments and research groups actually do. Therefore, a sample of those involved in visual computing is presented in the next section.

3.3   Research and Development in Visual Computing

A large number of corporations and universities have Visual Computing Groups involved in research and development in various topics. For illustrative purposes, a number of examples are included below.

Harvard University, USA, Visual Computing Group

The Visual Computing Group explores and provides visual analysis tools and methods to help scientists and researchers better process and understand large, multi-dimensional data sets in various domains such as neuroscience, genomics, systems biology, astronomy, and medicine [1]

Simon Fraser University, Canada, Visual Computing specialization
Simon Fraser University's School of Computing Science describes their program as:

> *Visual computing encompasses all computer science disciplines which study the acquisition, analysis, manipulation, and creation of 2D or 3D visual content. This includes computer graphics, computer vision, HCI, and visualization, serving numerous applications in design and manufacturing, education, medicine, geographical information systems, robotics, computer games, visual effects (VFX), as well as areas such as AR/VR/MR, autonomous driving, and 3D printing* [2].

King Abdullah University of Science and Technology (KAUST) Visual Computing Center (VCC)
KAUST summarizes its contributing disciplines to visual computing as follows:

> *KAUST VCC draws from expertise in multiple disciplines, including Computer Science, Electrical Engineering, Mechanical Engineering, and Applied Mathematics, as well as a range of application domains. This interdisciplinary view allows for a pipeline approach including device development (e.g. computational cameras and displays), image and video understanding and semantic analysis, geometric modeling and understanding, simulation, and visualization. By considering this whole pipeline, more effective solutions can be found for problems in the mentioned application domains.*

> *The Center serves as a focal point for interdisciplinary research, encompassing modeling, analysis, algorithm development, and simulation for problems arising throughout various fields in energy, environment, biosciences, earth sciences, materials science, and other disciplines* [3].

VCC performs large-scale visualizations, remote sensing, planning, and analysis of urban environments of the future by developing mathematical foundations, algorithms, and software.

Fraunhofer Institute for Computer Graphics (IGD)
Fraunhofer IGD summarizes its objectives as follows:

> *Fraunhofer IGD is the international leading research institution for applied visual computing — image- and model-based information technology that combines computer graphics and computer vision. In simple terms, it is the ability to turn information into images and to extract information from images. All technological solutions by Fraunhofer IGD and its partners are based on visual computing.*

> *In computer graphics, people generate, edit, and process images, graphs, and multidimensional models in a computer-aided manner. Examples are applications of virtual and simulated reality.*

> *Computer vision is the discipline that teaches computers how to »see«. In the process, a machine sees its environment by means of a camera and processes information using software. Typical applications can be found in the field of Augmented Reality* [4].

HTW Berlin, Visual Computing
The principal research interests are "*information retrieval, machine learning, visualization, computer vision, and visual clustering and sorting*" [5]. Current research topics include:

- *Optimization of deep learning frameworks*
- *Development of very compact image descriptors*

- *Visual sorting of millions of images using self-sorting maps and graphs*
- *Visualization and navigation schemes for graph-based image browsing*
- *Document segmentation (text/image)*
- *Automatic image tagging*
- *Image style analysis*
- *Image synthesis* [6].

Bonn-Rhein-Sieg University of Applied Sciences, Institute of Visual Computing
The principal research fields include:

- *Targeting Human Potential: Health, VR & Therapy, Low Latency Rendering, Photorealistic Rendering, Multi sensory interaction*
- *Exploiting Human Limitations: Perception driven Visualisation, Video Forensic*
- *Human Behaviour: Human Motion Analysis*
- *Digital Learning, Live Sciences & Education: Scientific Visualisation/VR/AR For Research and Education, Big Data, Machine Learning, Astronomy, Engineering Simulation, Hyperspectral Imaging*
- *Games Technology: 3D Simulation, Gamification* [7].

ETH Zurich, Visual Computing

The area of visual computing at ETH Zurich groups research activities in computer graphics, computer vision, geometry processing, human-computer interaction and visualization. Some of the key applications are in robotics, mobile communication, medical imaging, driver assistance, physical simulation as well as the film, game, and consumer electronics industries. In this area ETH Zurich particularly benefits from the close interaction with Disney Research Zurich.

Areas of research

animation, computer graphics, computer vision, game development, digital geometry processing, fabrication, human-computer interaction, imaging, video processing, visualization [8].

University of Rostock, Visual Computing and Computer Graphics (VCG)

VCG is concerned with all kinds of computer-based methods to deal with visual information. These methods include means to generate realistic images, to process image data, and to analyze data via visual representations. [9]

University of Bradford, UK, Centre for Visual Computing

The Centre has a unique dual focus. Research projects change the way we compute visual image data; our commercial projects address real business problems and deliver practical applications for our industry partners.

Core Research Areas

- *Electrodiagnostics*
- *Specialised Visual Assessments*
- *Ocular Imaging*
- *Machine Learning and Data Mining*
- *Human Visual Perception*

- *Computer Based Simulation*
- *Applied Digital Imaging*
- *Virtual Reality*
- *Visualisation* [10]

University of Bath, UK, Visual Computing
Research is performed at the intersection of computer vision and computer graphics [11].

Microsoft Visual Computing Group

> *The Visual Computing Group at Microsoft Research Asia consists of an elite team of researchers whose expertise spans the spectrum of research topics in computer vision, from mathematical theory to practical applications, from physical systems to software development, and from low-level image processing to high-level image understanding* [12].

Nvidia
Emphasizing the importance of the GPU, Nvidia state

> *Visual computing's power has simultaneously made it a tool for creation, a medium for artistic expression, and a platform for entertainment, exploration, and communications* [13].

Computer Graphics
Aspects of computer graphics are part of those of visual computing. The following computer graphics groups indicate some of the work being done in this area.

Stanford Computer Graphics
https://cs.stanford.edu/research/graphics
University of Washington Interactive Data Lab (visualization + analysis)
http://idl.cs.washington.edu/
University College, London, Virtual Environments and Computer Graphics
http://vecg.cs.ucl.ac.uk/
University of Freiburg
https://cg.informatik.uni-freiburg.de/
Bielefeld Graphics and Geometry Group
https://graphics.uni-bielefeld.de/
University of Bern Computer Graphics Group
http://cgg.unibe.ch/
URJC and UPM, Madrid, Modeling, and Virtual Reality Group
http://www.gmrv.es/index-old.php.

3.4 Conclusions

The components of visual computing have been reviewed. Different organizations and research groups concentrate on different aspects in order to align optimally with their expertise, and any applications that depend on the research outputs. In addition, institutions that are performing knowledge transfer have to synchronize with the requirements of their industrial partner(s). Other chapters in this book look at the components of large datasets and how to analyze them, the representations that can be used to display output data (visualization), and the application of analytical reasoning to the results facilitated by interactive visual interfaces (visual analytics).

Further Reading

Peters, J. F. Foundations of Computer Vision: Computational Geometry, Visual Image Structures and Object Shape Detection, Springer, Cham, Switzerland (2018). https://www.springer.com/gb/book/9783319524818

Bebis, J. Boyle, R. et al. (eds) Advances in Visual Computing: 13th International Symposium, ISVC 2018, Las Vegas, NV, USA, November 19–21, 2018, Proceedings. Springer, Cham, Switzerland (2018). https://www.springer.com/us/book/9783030038007, https://www.isvc.net/

Peddie, J. The History of Visual Magic in Computers: How Beautiful Images are Made in CAD, 3D, VR and AR, Springer, London (2013). https://www.springer.com/gb/book/9781447149316

Gross, M.H. Visual Computing—The Integration of Computer Graphics, Visual Perception and Imaging. Springer-Verlag Berlin Heidelberg (1994). https://www.springer.com/gp/book/9783642850257

References

1. https://vcg.seas.harvard.edu/
2. http://www.sfu.ca/computing/current-students/graduate-students/academic-programs/visual-computing.html
3. https://vcc.kaust.edu.sa/Pages/About.aspx
4. https://www.igd.fraunhofer.de/en
5. https://visual-computing.com/aboutus/
6. https://visual-computing.com/research/
7. http://vc.inf.h-bonn-rhein-sieg.de/
8. https://inf.ethz.ch/research/visual-computing.html
9. http://vcg.informatik.uni-rostock.de/en/
10. https://www.bradford.ac.uk/ei/media-design-technology/research/centre-for-visual-computing/
11. https://www.bath.ac.uk/projects/visual-computing/
12. https://www.microsoft.com/en-us/research/group/visual-computing/
13. https://www.nvidia.com/object/visual-computing.html

Chapter 4
Visualization

Rae Earnshaw

Abstract An overview of the principal aspects of visualization is provided. It presents an analysis of what visual tools and facilities are, and what they can do. These have developed over time and a summary of their history is also provided so that their present context in the analysis of data by computers can be more fully understood. Various aspects of computer graphics and visualization are reviewed, and a summary of current facilities in these areas is presented. The emphasis is on what these visual representations and tools can do rather than the current research and development that is taking place at the frontiers of the disciplines. However, references and further reading are provided for those who wish to drill down to the detail in a particular area. It is important also to consider the role that human perception and cognition plays in the understanding of images, their representations, and the colors that are used. The issue of appropriate use of images in representing data is considered, and the ownership and reproduction of images are reviewed. In order for a user to select particular parts of a dataset, or to zoom into an area of interest, appropriate interaction tools and facilities are needed. Using an interaction tool is a two-way process—it has to interface appropriately to the information space and the model being displayed by the computer, and also to the human using it. The human factors and ergonomics of using visual tools need to be considered, particularly in time-critical application areas. Professional societies and organizations in the area of visualization and their publication vehicles are summarized. Possible future directions for the display of visual information are reviewed.

Keywords Visual representation · Visual tools · Human vision system · Stereoscopic vision · Levels of abstraction · 2D and 3D visualizations · Image misuse · Copyright of images · Interaction tools · Interdisciplinary research and development · Perception of images · Human cognition · Simulation · Computer animation · Smart technology

© The Author(s), under exclusive license to Springer Nature Switzerland AG 2019   39
R. Earnshaw et al., *Data Science and Visual Computing*,
SpringerBriefs in Advanced Information and Knowledge Processing,
https://doi.org/10.1007/978-3-030-24367-8_4

4.1   Visual Representations

Visual representations have been used for centuries to display information or to understand concepts and principles, particularly in the arts and later in the physical sciences and engineering disciplines. In the former area, drawing, painting, and sculpture played a key role in expressing human creativity in reflections on the natural world. They were also used to directly express human imagination and individuality. The stereoscopic human vision system enables the physical world to be seen in 3D but many diagrammatic and artistic representations of the world which seek to do this in 2D do so in such a way that there is a perception of depth as far as a human viewer is concerned. This has the effect of making the image appear more realistic because it looks closer to reality.

An example of an early use of visualization is the march of Napoleon's Grand Army into Russia 18-12-13 and its retreat, and displaying the associated losses during the campaign [1].

The Scientific Revolution in the sixteenth and seventeenth centuries enabled a more systematic understanding of the natural world to be obtained. In particular, the laws by which it operated could be represented by numbers and mathematics which could be used to predict the ways in which the natural world would act or react. However, this was at a level of abstraction which could be difficult to understand, particularly when the mathematics became more complex. In order to more fully understand how these laws operated, it was generally regarded as useful to be able to represent the results of these calculations in visual form analogous to the ways in which the world could be seen to operate. Newton's Principia Mathematica [2] used many diagrams to illustrate the laws (e.g., gravity) by which Newton was seeking to define the natural world. Figure 4.1 shows an example where Newton was seeking to define the law of centripetal force directed to any point when an object moves in a circle (p76 of the English translation). It also assists subsequent researchers to more fully understand the structure of the argument being advanced and its strengths and weaknesses (e.g., Pourciau [3]).

4.2   Human Perception of Images

Humans see colors differently and do not necessarily see the same colors when they look at the same object. The same applies when looking at images on computer displays. The application of color theory to digital media and visualization has been considered in detail by Rhyne [4]. In addition, not all images convey the same messages to human viewers which has shifted the attention to human cognition and the need to take into account how the human visual system and the brain process the information that it receives and draws conclusions from it (Gregory [5]; Bodenheimer [6]; Gutierrez et al. [7]). The objective should be to illustrate the data, increase clarity, and enhance human understanding (Kostelnick [8]). In general, the facilities of

48 PHILOSOPHIÆ NATURALIS.

Dɪ Motu Corpokum.

Corol. 4. Iifdem pofitis, eſt vis centripeta ut velocitas bis directe, & chorda illa inverfe. Nam velocitas eſt reciproce ut perpendiculum *ST* per corol. 1. prop. 1.

Corol. 5. Hinc fi detur figura quævis curvilinea *APQ*, & in ea detur etiam punctum *S*, ad quod vis centripeta perpetuo dirigitur, inveniri poteſt lex vis centripetæ, qua corpus quodvis *P* a curfu rectilineo perpetuo retractum in figuræ illius perimetro detinebitur, eamque revolvendo defcribet. Nimirum computandum eſt vel folidum $\frac{SPq \times QTq}{QR}$ vel folidum STq × *PV* huic vi reciproce proportionale. Ejus rei dabimus exempla in problematis fequentibus.

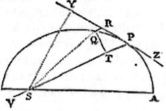

PROPOSITIO VII. PROBLEMA II.

Gyretur corpus in circumferentia circuli, requiritur lex vis centripetæ tendentis ad punctum quodcunque datum.

Eſto circuli circumferentia *VQPA*; punctum datum, ad quod vis ceu ad centrum fuum tendit, *S*; corpus in circumferentia latum *P*; locus proximus, in quem movebitur *Q*; & circuli tangens ad locum priorem *PRZ*. Per punctum *S* ducatur chorda *PV*; & acta circuli diametro *VA*, jungatur *AP*; & ad *SP* demittatur perpendiculum *QT*, quod productum occurrat tangenti *PR* in *Z*; ac denique per punctum *Q* agatur *LR*, quæ ipfi *SP* parallella fit, & occurrat tum circulo in *L*, tum tangenti *PZ* in *R*. Et ob fimilia triangula *ZQR*, *ZTP*, *VPA*; erit *RP. quad.* hoc eſt QRL ad QT quad.

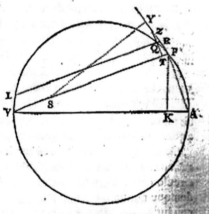

8

Fig. 4.1 A page from Principia Mathematica showing the use of diagrams to illustrate the principles. By Isaac Newton (Public domain), via Wikimedia Commons https://commons.wikimedia.org/w/index.php?curid=29543

visual representation support this goal when used by people who understand how to use them for different types of data and information (Tufte [9, 10]). Data and information can be processed using appropriate software and then displayed using a particular visual representation. Much work has been done in the latter area to ensure that the visual image is a useful and adequate representation of the underlying data and information, and enables the viewer to gain insight into the data (Brown et al. [11]; Carlson [12]; Friendly [13]; Peddie [14]). According to Hamming [15], this is the primary purpose of computing.

4.3   Use and Misuse of Images

There have been concerns about the use of graphs and charts to misrepresent data whether accidentally or deliberately (Parikh [16]; Esteban [17]; Jones [18]). Examples include inappropriate scaling of axes, comparing two graphs with different axes, and stating that correlation implies a causal relationship. One of the issues with such representations is that they can be displayed quickly in a presentation, or in a television program, to convey a particular point. The observer does not have time to check whether the point being made is valid and may just assume that the visuals are appropriate because they are representing the data in an easily assimilated form. This is a point to bear in mind when products and services are being compared in promotional advertising, or during political campaigning which seeks to influence the public's decision-making processes, or when researchers are under pressure to produce results to meet a project or publication deadline. This raises the issue of ethics in the accurate presentation of data (Marco and Larkin [19]; Coultas [20]; Daniels [21]), and the need for publishers, reviewers, and the media to validate and ensure the integrity and soundness of information submitted to them (Newton [22]; Bishop [23]; Boucherie [24]). Journals have had to retract papers when it has subsequently been found that the data are inaccurate, inappropriately presented, or fabricated. In one case, there was alleged image manipulation in the published papers (The Scientist [25]). The Committee on Publication Ethics (COPE [26]) seeks to promote integrity in research and its publication. With the rise of communication by social media, there is also a need to consider the responsibilities of disseminators and receivers of information in this environment (Bishop and Gray [27]).

4.4   Ownership and Reproduction of Images

With the proliferation of mobile phones with digital cameras, the issue frequently arises of who owns the digital image when a photograph is taken. Generally, this is the originator of the image (assuming it is a photograph of a public place or space), unless part of the content of the image is another image subject to copyright (e.g., an artwork in an art gallery which is owned by someone else). In this case, the permission of the owner of the copyright needs to be obtained. The UK government's Intellectual Property Office (IPO) has issued guidelines with regard to digital images, photographs, and the Internet [28].

Images may have a Creative Commons Licence which grants permission to reuse (e.g., copy, share, remix, transform, and build upon) with appropriate acknowledgements as defined in association with the original image. This includes CC-0 which does not need attribution, CC-BY which needs attribution, and CC-BY-NC which indicates free for noncommercial reuse. The Advanced Search option in Google Images enables images to be filtered by Usage Rights.

4.5 Interaction

So far the production of an image has been regarded as a passive process. The data are selected or generated, they are processed, a representation is selected, and the image is displayed on an appropriate device. This would apply equally to an artistic or computational process. Interaction allows a user to input more directly into the formation of the image and is normally a combination of hardware and software. Aspects of interaction include the following:

1. Selection of a portion of the current image in order to focus on a particular area,
2. Input some additional information to the data in order to refine the image,
3. Steer the computation process to concentrate on different parts of the dataset, and
4. Explore different areas of the displayed 3D space, such as those in a virtual reality environment.

Interaction is mandatory for virtual reality environments because the movement of the user's head and eyes causes the view of the scene to change as the position and orientation of the user's head and eyes change, and thus the user is de facto interacting with the image. Therefore, the position and direction of view of the user's head (and possibly also eyes in some cases) need to be tracked in real time so that the appropriate view of the scene can be generated and displayed. Interaction normally also requires some form of device for the user to indicate their intentions with regard to what is being displayed. There are many kinds of devices with different ergonomic properties. In 2D, an input device can select, point, or input a command via clicking a button, performing a gesture on a device, or providing speech input. In 3D, the tasks involve selection and manipulation, navigation, symbolic input, and system control. Studies in this field are under the general theme of "Human–Computer Interaction" (HCI) (Shneiderman et al. [29]; Sharp et al. [30]; Hughes et al. [31]; Buxton [32]; Yi et al. [33]; Endert et al. [34]).

4.6 Computer Graphics

Computer graphics uses computer hardware and software to produce images on displays (Hughes et al. [35]). It is often known as Computer Generated Imagery (CGI). It can be used to process and display data from the physical world (e.g., from scientific experiments or from sensors) as well as generating artificial scenes for design, animation, and special effects. One of the goals of computer graphics has been to create images with textures and light reflections which enhance their realism from a human point of view. An understanding of the laws of physics is useful in achieving this goal. A variety of techniques have been developed in software to produce realistic images, many of which are available for free download. Examples of these are included in Table 4.1. They may also be bundled into commercial software where a vendor is targeting a particular application domain (e.g., computer-aided design).

The development of computer graphics in the period 1970–2000 came at a time when hardware was increasing in power, functionality, and diversity. Graphics work-stations could perform the calculations required to produce the images, and software was developed to allow high-level programs to be written to interface the application to the hardware. With the continuing increase in computer power, such functionality can now be embedded in a graphics card and used in a PC. In addition, high-speed networks can transport the results of detailed calculations on complex and large datasets from supercomputers, and then display them on portable devices such as tablets and mobile phones.

Computer graphics depends on advancements in computer science for its hard-ware, software, and networking and also on geometry for representing models, optics for ensuring light is correctly represented, and physics for making objects move according to scientific laws. The latter is particularly relevant for computer anima-tions for films and video games (Parent, 2012). Objects in an animation are not believable unless they move in the same way as they are known to move in the real world. Thus, they need to conform to the characteristics of the physical world.

4.7 Visualizing with Images

Visualization uses images to communicate a particular result or message, or to enable an observer to explore different aspects of the dataset in order to gain a better under-standing of its significance (Ward [36]; Munzner [37]). Although visualization tools were developed later on in the history of computer graphics, it could be argued that visualization as a concept preceded computer graphics since it can be independent of computing technology. However, it becomes particularly powerful when utilizing interactive computer graphics hardware and software. The various kinds of visual-izations that can be considered depending on the particular objective, for example, comparing the data with other datasets, or showing the relationship between different

Table 4.1 Examples of data visualization software (further software is in Chap. 6, Table 6.1)

Software	Developer	Application Areas	Web site	Date
Avizo	FEI Visualization Sciences Group	Scientific and industrial data visualization and analysis	www.vsg3d.com	2016
Baudline	SigBlips DSP Engineering	Signal analysis tool designed for scientific visualization	www.baudline.com	2000
Bitplane	Andor Technology/Oxford Instruments	3D and 4D image analysis for the life sciences	www.bitplane.com	1992
Datacopia	Datacopia	Generates charts and infographics from structured and unstructured data	www.datacopia.com	2012
Dataplot	National Institute of Standards and Technology	Public-domain software system for scientific visualization and statistical analysis	Not known	Not known
DataMelt	Dr. Sergei V. Chekanov	Interactive framework for scientific computation	jwork.org/dmelt/	2017
MeVisLab	MeVis Medical Solutions AG	Medical image processing and scientific visualization	www.mevislab.de	2016
NCAR Command Language	National Center for Atmospheric Research	Atmospheric research	ncar.ucar.edu	
Orange	University of Ljubljana	Open-source data visualization, machine learning, and data mining toolkit	orange.biolab.si	1997
ParaView	Sandia National Laboratory, Kitware Inc, Los Alamos National Laboratory	Open-source multiple-platform application for interactive, scientific visualization	www.paraview.org	2016

(continued)

Table 4.1 (continued)

Software	Developer	Application Areas	Web site	Date
Tecplot	Tecplot Inc	Comparing collections of CFD simulations	www.tecplot.com	2016
tomviz	Not known	Open-source software platform for reproducible volumetric visualization and data processing	www.tomviz.com	2014
VAPOR	National Center for Atmospheric Research	Produce images and movies from very large mesh-based datasets	https://www.vapor.ucar.edu/	2016
Vis5D	Not known	Open-source animated 3D visualization of weather simulations	http://www.ssec.wisc.edu/~billh/vis5d.html	1989
VisAD	Not known	Open-source interactive and collaborative visualization and analysis of numerical data	http://www.ssec.wisc.edu/~billh/visad.html	Not known
VisIt	Lawrence Livermore National Laboratory	Open-source interactive parallel visualization and graphical analysis tool for viewing very large dataset sizes in the terascale range	visit.llnl.gov	Not known
VTK	Kitware Inc.	Open-source supports a wide variety of visualization algorithms including scalar, vector, tensor, texture, and volumetric methods; and advanced modeling techniques such as implicit modeling, polygon reduction, mesh smoothing, cutting, contouring, and Delaunay triangulation	www.vtk.org	2017

(continued)

Table 4.1 (continued)

Software	Developer	Application Areas	Web site	Date
Category: Free data visualization software	Various	List of open-source, data visualization software which can be freely used, copied, studied, modified, and redistributed by everyone that obtains a copy	Not known	Not known

parts of the data, or compiling a set of graphs for a presentation, or illustrating the distributions in the data for publication [38]. Visualization can assist in collaborative design and also in optimizing designs [39–41].

4.8 Scientific Visualization

Scientific visualization rose to prominence as a particular aspect of general visualization when graphics workstations and supercomputer hardware and software became available which was capable of analyzing large and complex datasets. These were being produced from scientific experiments, or from real-time sensors monitoring the natural world or astrophysical events (Earnshaw and Wiseman [42]). It was initiated in the USA in 1987 principally by a report from a panel on *Graphics, Image Processing and Workstations to provide input to the National Science Foundation's Division of Advanced Scientific Computing on how best to utilize supercomputers to meet users' needs in a variety of scientific disciplines. This report, Visualization in Scientific Computing* (McCormick et al. [43]), *described how such an initiative could be accomplished, and has provided the basis for much of the subsequent development in this field. Although this initiative was first driven by the needs and requirements of scientific users, it is clear in retrospect that the strategies and methods used can be applied in many other disciplines. Arts and humanities research projects can produce significant amounts of data (e.g., in the analysis of manuscripts)* (Graham [44]). *The term "scientific" was attached to visualization because many of the first users with research grants who were processing their data on supercomputers needed facilities for analyzing and interpreting their results in the physical and biological sciences. The term "data visualization" is currently more often used to include all disciplines where data analysis is required, and the label "scientific" has been largely dropped.*

Figure 4.2 shows a visualization of car deformation in a collision. The objective in this simulation is to ascertain where the greatest stresses occur, so that these areas and components can be strengthened in order to provide greater protection.

Examples of Data Visualization software with their application areas are summarized in Table 4.1.

The software items listed in Table 4.1 are courtesy of the Wikipedia site https://en.wikipedia.org/wiki/Scientific_visualization.

4.9 Information Visualization

Information visualization is a particular category of visualization where the visual representation is chosen by the particular system being used, and where the data may be abstract in nature (Card et al. [45]; Bederson and Shneiderman [46]; Spence [47]; Ware [48]; Borkin [49]; Rogowitz [50]). It can contain numerical and non-numerical data. The spatial representation of the information on a screen can be varied to suit

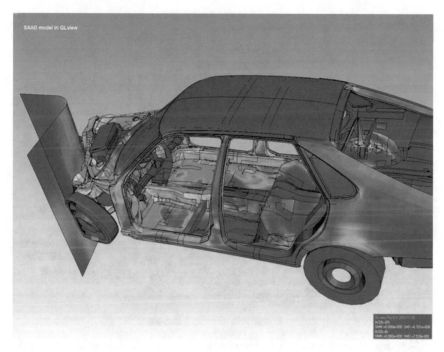

Fig. 4.2 Visualization of how a car deforms in an asymmetrical crash using finite element analysis (Image in the public domain, https://commons.wikimedia.org/w/index.php?curid=641911)

user goals and is not tied to any particular underlying geometry as is often the case for scientific visualization. Thus, it differs from scientific visualization where the spatial representation is normally defined by the data. Figure 4.3 shows how information can be represented using symbols and links.

4.10 Communities and Publications

One of the first groups on computer graphics and interactive techniques was founded in 1969 in the USA by ACM and hosts an annual international conference (with the first one in 1974). The research papers were originally published as conference proceedings but from 2003 they now appear as a special issue of the ACM Transactions on Graphics which is a refereed journal for papers in the general areas of computer graphics hardware, software, and techniques. In the past, applications have not received much attention because the conference is driven primarily by academic researchers in universities and research laboratories. Application papers are published in IEEE Computer Graphics & Applications. ACM Siggraph's Mission Statement is as follows:

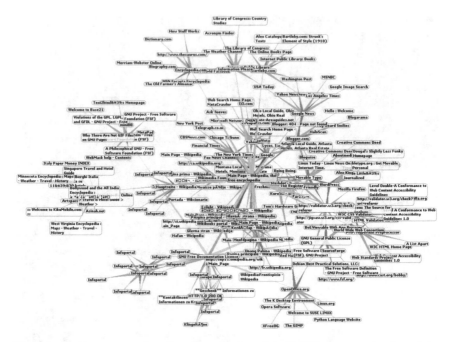

Fig. 4.3 Graphic representation of a minute fraction of the WWW, demonstrating hyperlinks. Permission is granted to copy, distribute, and/or modify this document under the terms of the GNU Free Documentation License, Version 1.3. This Wikipedia and Wikimedia Commons image is from the user Chris 73 and is freely available at https://commons.wikimedia.org/wiki/File: WorldWideWebAroundWikipedia.png under the creative commons cc-by-sa 3.0 license

> *ACM SIGGRAPH's mission is to foster and celebrate innovation in Computer Graphics and Interactive Techniques. The organization promotes its vision by bringing people together in physical, on-line, and asynchronous communities to invent, inspire, and redefine the many creative and technical artifacts, disciplines, and industries that are touched by computer graphics and interactive techniques.*

An IEEE Visualization conference was started in 1990 and the proceedings were published in the Transactions on Computer Graphics and Visualization from 2006. Its principal areas are scientific visualization, information visualization, and visual analytics. Isenberg et al. [51] describe, using visualizations, all the papers published up to 2017 at the Visualization conferences. The IEEE Visualization community does not have a specific mission except the objectives associated with its Visualization and Graphics Technical Committee (VGTC) which is as follows:

> *The IEEE Computer Society Technical Committee on Visualization and Graphics (VGTC) promotes research in computer graphics, visualization, and virtual reality as well as the application of these topics to science, engineering, business, and the arts. Research interests include hardware, software, algorithms, and user interfaces. Specific topics of emphasis within VGTC are visualization, computer graphics, and virtual reality.*

The mission of the IEEE organization is as follows:

IEEE's core purpose is to foster technological innovation and excellence for the benefit of humanity.

Another group concentrating on human–computer interaction was set up in the USA by ACM in 1982 and this also has an annual conference with proceedings. Its mission statement is as follows:

ACM SIGCHI is the leading international community of professionals interested in research, education and the practical application of human-computer interaction. We enable our members to create and shape how people interact with technology and understand how technologies have an impact in people's lives.

Numerous other national and international conferences and journals have publications in the areas of graphics and visualization, and a number of these are included in the list of professional societies and organizations below.

4.11 Professional Societies, Organizations, and Associated Publications

ACM Siggraph
https://en.wikipedia.org/wiki/ACM_SIGGRAPH
Mission Statement
https://www.siggraph.org/about/mission-and-vision
ACM Siggraph History
https://www.siggraph.org/about/history
ACM Transactions on Graphics (TOG)
https://en.wikipedia.org/wiki/ACM_Transactions_on_Graphics
IEEE Visualization
https://en.wikipedia.org/wiki/IEEE_Visualization
IEEE Transactions on Visualization and Computer Graphics (TVCG)
https://en.wikipedia.org/wiki/IEEE_Transactions_on_Visualization_and_
Computer_Graphics
Objectives of the VGTC Committee
https://www.ieee.org/membership-catalog/productdetail/showProductDetailPage.
html?product=CMYVG731
IEEE Mission
https://www.ieee.org/about/vision-mission.html
IEEE Computer Graphics & Applications (CG&A)
https://www.ieee.org/membership-catalog/productdetail/showProductDetailPage.
html?product=PER306-ELE&refProd=MEMC016
ACM Symposium on Interactive 3D Graphics and Games (I3DG)
http://i3dsymposium.github.io/2018/
ACM Human–Computer Interaction (HCI)

https://sigchi.org/
Mission Statement: https://sigchi.org/about/mission-statement/
IEEE Pacific Visualization Conference (IEEE PacVis)
http://www.wikicfp.com/cfp/program?id=2286&f=IEEE
CG International (CGS)
http://www.cgs-network.org/cgi18/
International Conference on Computers and Games
https://link.springer.com/conference/cg
ACM SIGGRAPH/Eurographics Symposium on Computer Animation (SCA)
http://research.cbs.chula.ac.th/pvis2019/home.aspx
Eurographics Symposium on Geometry Processing (SGP)
https://sgp2018.sciencesconf.org/
Pacific Graphics Conference (PG)
http://www.wikicfp.com/cfp/program?id=2353&s=PG&f=Pacific%
20Conference%20on%20Computer%20Graphics%20and%20Applications
Eurovis—The EG and VGTC Conference on Visualization
http://vgtc.org/archives/eurovis
Graphics Interfaces (GI)
http://graphicsinterface.org/
Optical Society of America (OSA)
https://www.osa.org/en-us/home/
Society for Information Display (SID)
https://www.sid.org/
International Society for Optics and Photonics (SPIE)
http://spie.org/?SSO=1
Society for Imaging Science and Technology (IS&T)
https://www.imaging.org/site/ist

4.12   Current and Future Directions in Computer Analysis and Display

The development of the computer and associated information technology has increased the utilization and application of visual tools in many application areas. Their use is now ubiquitous and many people use the facilities in many other contexts (e.g., social media) without needing to understand how images are produced and transported.

There are a number of reasons why the current interest in digital imaging is increasing. These include the following:

- Availability of higher resolution displays;
- Increasing use of virtual reality devices for research, development, personal assistance, and entertainment;

- Portable screens and cameras in mobile phones, and possible flexible screens;
- Rapid image generation to meet specific application area requirements (e.g., the need to make a quick decision in a real-time emergency situation);
- Faster networks;
- Reducing cost;
- Handling copyright and watermarking issues in digital images; and
- Human perception and cognition issues associated with viewing and interacting with images and display devices.

The latter area—human perception and cognition—might be assumed to be insignificant, or not relevant, because it is invisible to the human eye and not consciously recognized by the human brain. Yet, it governs all aspects of how we understand and interpret images and interact with them. Just as humans see colors differently for various reasons, so they see and interact with images differently.

Current research and development on displays is at the intersection of computer graphics, optics, human perception, and cognition. Examples are light field displays, thin transparency displays (e.g., Lumii), stacked LCD displays, near-eye displays, and non-line-of-sight imaging (O'Toole et al. [52]). A computational approach to display design is facilitating new classes of displays. For example, a vision-correcting display enables a person's eyeglasses to be functionally embedded in the display rather than placed on the user's head (Huang et al. [53]).

In an Awards presentation at ACM Siggraph 2018, Wetzstein [54] summarized current research and development work at the intersection of computer graphics, machine vision, optics, scientific computing, and perception, and indicated that this interdisciplinary work required cross-fertilization with that of other research communities in areas such as optics, display, and imaging science. It is likely that this kind of interdisciplinary research will increase in the future because of the overall needs and requirements of the field. An example of this is the current collaborations between art, design, and technology (Earnshaw [55]). There is also an increasing use of machine learning in image editing tools, 3D rendering products, and video stylization (Agrawal [56]). In addition, computer graphics is being used in the area of very large models and also more complex simulations, which are both areas of big data challenges.

The way humans interact with machines in general and visual displays in particular is a complex area. One possible way forward is to decrease the amount of direct interaction (and therefore the demands on a user's attention and cognitive processes) and embed smart computing technology into the environment where it gains more of its input from automatic sensors. This approach can be utilized in the Internet of Things (Greengard [57]; Miller [58]; Marr [59]). Other ways are seeking to produce interaction devices and environments which are more natural, user-friendly, and directly meeting human requirements (Earnshaw [60]).

4.13 Conclusions

This chapter has reviewed key aspects in the development of visualization from the earliest forms of pictorial representations. The advent of computers initiated a more systematic way of processing data and presenting the results in graphical form. Further developments in hardware, including the supercomputer, raised the issue of what to do with the "fire-hoses" of information that were being produced from computational processing of data. How can all this be analyzed effectively and appropriate decisions made? This produced visualization environments and software to enable humans to understand the meaning of the data. This generated a further shift toward a focus on human perception and cognition and how the processes of viewing and interacting with visual images can be best understood. Further information on geometric primitives and geometric visualization, and visual analytics science and technology are provided in later chapters in this volume.

It is important therefore to recognize the benefits and advances that the development of this subject area has brought to the academy, industry, and the community. At the same time, it is also important not to be locked into the history of the subject, nor the ways in which it is currently being organized and developed, but to be open to new ideas, paradigms, and directions, which will further human understanding and application of visualization.

Further Reading

Tierny, J. Topological Data Analysis for Scientific Visualization, Springer, Cham Switzerland (2018). https://www.springer.com/gb/book/9783319715063

Moller, T. Hamann, B. Russell, R. Mathematical Foundations of Scientific Visualization, Computer Graphics, and Massive Data Exploration, Springer, Cham, Switzerland (2010). https://www.springer.com/gb/book/9783540250760

Hansen, C. Chen, M. Johnson, C.R. Kaufman, A.E. Hagen, H. Scientific Visualization: Uncertainty, Multifield, Biomedical, and Scalable Visualization, Springer, Cham, Switzerland (2014). https://www.springer.com/gb/book/9781447164968

Bethel, E.W. Childs, H. Hansen, C. High Performance Visualization: Enabling Extreme-Scale Scientific Insight, CRC Press/Chapman and Hall, Boca Raton, FL (2012, hardback), (2016, paperback). https://www.crcpress.com/High-Performance-Visualization-Enabling-Extreme-Scale-Scientific-Insight/Bethel-Childs-Hansen/p/book/9781138199613

Chen, M. Feixas, M. Viola, I. Bardera, A. Shen, H.W. Sbert, M. Information Theory Tools for Visualization, CRC Press, Boca Raton, FL (2016). https://www.crcpress.com/Information-Theory-Tools-for-Visualization/Chen-Feixas-Viola-Bardera-Shen-Sbert/p/book/9781498740937

References

1. https://bigthink.com/strange-maps/229-vital-statistics-of-a-deadly-campaign-the-minard-map
2. Newton, I., Cohen, I.B., Whitman, A.: The Principia: The Authoritative Translation: Mathematical Principles of Natural Philosophy. University of California Press, CA (2016) (originally published in Latin, 1687)
3. Pourciau, B.: Force, deflection, and time: proposition VI of Newton's Principia. Hist. Math. **34**, 140–172 (2007). https://www.sciencedirect.com/science/article/pii/S0315086006000930
4. Rhyne, T.M.: Applying Color Theory to Digital Media and Visualization. CRC Press, Boca Raton, FL (2016)
5. Gregory, R.: Eye and Brain: The Psychology of Seeing, 5th edn. Oxford University Press (1997)
6. Bodenheimer, B.: Computer Graphics and the Visual System (2018). https://pdfs.semanticscholar.org/presentation/c444/a95e7d0876d27d5748f2215f150d19b83612.pdf
7. Gutierrez, D., Anson, O., Seron, F.J., Muñoz, A., Jimenez, E.: The Human Visual System as the next step in Virtual Reality. https://www.researchgate.net/publication/228849092_THE_HUMAN_VISUAL_SYSTEM_AS_THE_NEXT_STEP_IN_VIRTUAL_REALITY
8. Kostelnick, C.: The visual rhetoric of data displays: the conundrum of clarit. IEEE Trans. Prof. Commun. **50**(4), 280–294 (2007) (IEEE, New York, NY)
9. Tufte, E.R.: The Visual Display of Quantitative Information, 2nd edn. Graphics Press, Cheshire, CT (2001)
10. Tufte, E.R.: Envisioning Information. Graphics Press, Cheshire, CT (1990)
11. Brown, J.R., Earnshaw, R.A., Jern, M., Vince, J.A.: Visualization: Using Computer Graphics to Explore Data and Present Information. Wiley, Hoboken, NJ (1995). ISBN 0-471-12991-7. http://www.amazon.co.uk/Visualization-Computer-Graphics-Explore-Information/dp/0471129917
12. Carlson, W.: A Critical History of Computer Graphics and Animation (2003). https://web.archive.org/web/20070405172134/http://accad.osu.edu/~waynec/history/lessons.html, http://accad.osu.edu/~waynec/history/lessons.html
13. Friendly, M.: Milestones in the history of thematic cartography, statistical graphics, and data visualization, p. 79 (2009). http://www.math.yorku.ca/SCS/Gallery/milestone/milestone.pdf
14. Peddie, J.: The History of Visual Magic in Computers: How Beautiful Images are Made in CAD, 3D, VR and AR. Springer, Cham, Switzerland (2013)
15. Hamming, R.W.: Numerical Methods for Scientists and Engineers. Dover Publications Inc., Mineola, NY (1987) (first published 1962)
16. Parikh, R.: How to Lie with Data Visualization (2014). https://heapanalytics.com/blog/data-stories/how-to-lie-with-data-visualization
17. Esteban, C.: A Quick Guide to Spotting Graphics that Lie, National Geographic, June 19, Washington, DC (2015). https://news.nationalgeographic.com/2015/06/150619-data-points-five-ways-to-lie-with-charts/
18. Jones, A.: How to Lie with Visualizations: Statistics, Causation vs Correlation, and Intuition! Data Science Central (2015). https://www.datasciencecentral.com/profiles/blogs/how-to-lie-with-visualizations-statistics-causation-vs
19. Marco, C.A., Larkin, G.L.: Research ethics: ethical issues of data reporting and the quest for authenticity. Acad. Emerg. Med. **7**(6), 691–694 (2000). https://onlinelibrary.wiley.com/doi/pdf/10.1111/j.1553-2712.2000.tb02049.x
20. Coultas, D.: Ethical considerations in the interpretation and communication of clinical trial results. Proc. Am. Thorac. Soc. **4**(1) (2007). https://www.atsjournals.org/doi/full/10.1513/pats.200701-007GC
21. Daniels, D.: Exploring ethical issues when using visual tools in educational research. In: Liamputtong, P. (ed.) Doing Cross-Cultural Research Ethical and Methodological Perspectives, pp. 119–133. Springer, Cham, Switzerland (2008). https://link.springer.com/chapter/10.1007/978-1-4020-8567-3_9

22. Newton, J.J.: Chapter 23 visual representation of people and information: translating lives into numbers, words, and images as research data. In: Mertens, D.M., Ginsberg, P.E. (eds.) The Handbook of Social Research Ethics. Sage, Thousand Oaks, CA (2009). http://methods. sagepub.com/Book/the-handbook-of-social-research-ethics/n23.xml
23. Bishop, L.: Legal and Ethical Issues in Data Sharing (2015) (slide presentation). https://www. ukdataservice.ac.uk/media/604103/5rdm_manchester2015_legalethical.pdf
24. Boucherie, S.: "Predatory" vs trustworthy journals: what do they mean for the integrity of science? Elsevier Connect, Amsterdam, NL (2018). https://www.elsevier.com/connect/predatory-vs-trustworthy-journals-what-do-they-mean-for-the-integrity-of-science
25. The Scientist. https://www.the-scientist.com/research-round-up/top-10-retractions-of-2017-29834, https://retractionwatch.com/2017/05/25/journal-retracts-nine-papers-one-day-author-investigation-weizmann-institute/ (2017)
26. Committee on Publication Ethics (COPE). https://publicationethics.org/
27. Bishop, L., Gray, D.: Chapter 7 ethical challenges of publishing and sharing social media research data. In: Woodfield, K. (ed.) The Ethics of Online Research (Advances in Research Ethics and Integrity, vol. 2), pp. 159–187. Emerald Publishing Limited, Bingley, UK (2017). https://www.emeraldinsight.com/doi/abs/10.1108/S2398-601820180000002007
28. IPO: Copyright Notice: Digital Images, Photographs and the Internet (2015). https://assets. publishing.service.gov.uk/government/uploads/system/uploads/attachment_data/file/481194/ c-notice-201401.pdf
29. Shneiderman, B., Plaisant, Cohen, M., Jacobs, S., Elmqvist, N.: Designing the User Interface: Strategies for Effective Human Computer Interaction, 6th edn. Pearson, London, UK (2017)
30. Sharp, H., Preece, J., Rogers, Y.: Interaction Design: Beyond Human-Computer Interaction, 5th edn. Wiley, Hoboken, NJ (2019)
31. Chapter 21 Interaction Techniques. In: Hughes, J.F., van Dam, A., McGuire, M., Sklar, D.F., Foley J.D., Feiner, S.K., Akeley, K. (eds.) Computer Graphics: Principles and Practice, 3rd edn, pp. 567–594. Addison Wesley, Boston, MA (2013)
32. Buxton, W.: Input and Interactive Devices. https://www.microsoft.com/buxtoncollection
33. Yi, J.S., ah Kang, Y., Stasko, J.: Toward a deeper understanding of the role of interaction in information visualization. IEEE Trans. Vis. Comput. Graph. 13(6), 1224–1231 (2007). https:// ieeexplore.ieee.org/document/4376144
34. Endert, A., Ribarsky, W., Turkay, C., Wong, B.W., Nabney, I., Blanco, I.D., Rossi, F.: The state of the art in integrating machine learning into visual analytics. Comput. Graph. Forum 36(8), 458–486 (2017). https://onlinelibrary.wiley.com/doi/abs/10.1111/cgf.13092
35. Hughes, J.F., van Dam, A., McGuire, M., Sklar, D.F., Foley J.D., Feiner, S.K., Akeley, K.: Computer Graphics: Principles and Practice, 3rd edn, p. 1264. Addison Wesley, Boston, MA (2013)
36. Ward, M.O., Grinstein, G., Keim, D.: Interactive Data Visualization: Foundations, Techniques, and Applications, p. 513. A. K. Peters/CRC Press, Boca Raton, FL (2010)
37. Munzner, T.M.: Visualization Analysis and Design. CRC Press, Boca Raton, FL (2014)
38. https://towardsdatascience.com/5-quick-and-easy-data-visualizations-in-python-with-code-a2284bae952f
39. https://visualizingarchitecture.com/interior-elevations-tutorial-video/
40. Mulloni, A., Nadalutti, D., Chittaro, L.: Interactive walkthrough of large 3D models of buildings on mobile devices. In: Proceedings of the 12th International Conference on 3D Web Technology (Web3D07), pp. 17–25. ACM, New York (2007). https://dl.acm.org/citation.cfm? doid=1229390.1229393
41. Lamotte, W., Earnshaw, R.A., Van Reeth, F., Flerackers, E., Mena De Matos, J.: VISINET: collaborative 3D visualization and virtual reality over trans-European ATM networks. IEEE Comput. Graph. Appl. (Special Issue on 3D and Multimedia on the Information Superhighway) 17(2), 66–75 (1997) (IEEE, Los Alamitos, CA). http://www.computer.org/portal/web/csdl/doi/ 10.1109/38.574684. http://doi.ieeecomputersociety.org/10.1109/38.574684
42. Earnshaw, R.A., Wiseman, N.: An Introductory Guide to Scientific Visualization. Springer, Berlin, Heidelberg (1992). ISBN 0-387-54664-2 (Foreword by Dr. James H. Clark, pp. v–vi). http://link.springer.com/book/10.1007/978-3-642-58101-4

43. McCormick, B.H., de Fanti, T.A., Brown, M.D.: Visualization in scientific computing. Comput. Graph. **21**(6) (1987) (ACM Siggraph, ACM, New York). https://www.evl.uic.edu/core.php?mod=4&type=3&indi=348

44. Graham, E.: Introduction: data visualisation and the humanities. J. Engl. Stud. **98**(5), 449–458 (2017) (Taylor and Francis Online, Abingdon, UK). https://www.tandfonline.com/doi/full/10.1080/0013838X.2017.1332021

45. Card, S., Mackinlay, J.D., Shneiderman, B.: Readings in Information Visualization: Using Vision to Think. Morgan Kaufmann, San Francisco, CA (1999)

46. Bederson, B., Shneiderman, B.: The Craft of Information Visualization: Readings and Reflections. Morgan Kaufmann, San Francisco, CA (2003)

47. Spence, R.: Information Visualization: Design for Interaction, 2nd edn. Prentice Hall, New York, NY (2007). ISBN 0-13-206550-9

48. Ware, C.: Information Visualization: Perception for Design, Morgan Kaufmann, 3rd edn. Burlington, MA (2012)

49. Borkin, M.A.: Perception, cognition, and effectiveness of visualizations with applications in science and engineering. Doctoral dissertation, Harvard University, Cambridge, MA (2014). https://dash.harvard.edu/handle/1/12274335

50. Rogowitz, B.: Nuggets of Wisdom from Research in Perception and Cognition: A Guide for Visualization and Imaging. Morgan & Claypool, San Rafael, CA (2019)

51. Isenberg, P., Heimerl, F., Koch, S., Isenberg, T., Xu, P., Stolper, C., Sedlmair, M., Chen, J., Möller, T., Stasko, J.: vispubdata.org: a metadata collection about IEEE visualization (VIS) publications. IEEE Trans. Vis. Comput. Graph. **23**(9), 2199–2206 (2017) (IEEE, Los Alamitos, CA). https://hal.inria.fr/hal-01376597/document

52. O'Toole, M., Lindell, D., Wetzstein, G.: Confocal non-line-of-sight imaging based on the light-cone transform. Nature **555**, 338–341 (2018) (London, UK). Editor's summary: "Shining light on the out of sight". https://www.nature.com/articles/nature25489?WT.feed_name=subjects_imaging-and-sensing, http://www.computationalimaging.org/publications/confocal-non-line-of-sight-imaging-based-on-the-light-cone-transform/

53. Huang, F.C., Wetzstein, G., Barsky, B., Raskar, R.L.: Eyeglasses-free display: towards correcting visual aberrations with computational light field displays. ACM Trans. Graph. **33**(4) (2014) (New York, NY)

54. Wetzstein, G.: ACM Siggraph Awards 2018 presentation. https://www.youtube.com/watch?v=MkluiD2lYCc. Starts around 43 mins in, and finishes at around 61 mins

55. Earnshaw, R.A.: Art, Design and Technology: Collaboration and Implementation. Springer, Cham, Switzerland (2017). http://www.springer.com/gp/book/9783319581200

56. Agrawal, A.: Application of machine learning to computer graphics. IEEE Comput. Graph. Appl. **38**(4), 93–96 (2018) (IEEE, Los Alamitos, CA). https://ieeexplore.ieee.org/document/8402157

57. Greengard, S.: The Internet of Things. MIT Press, Cambridge, MA (2015)

58. Miller, M.: The Internet of Things: How Smart TVs, Smart Cars, Smart Homes, and Smart Cities are changing the World, QUE, Indianapolis, IN (2015). http://ptgmedia.pearsoncmg.com/images/9780789754004/samplepages/9780789754004.pdf

59. Marr, B.: Data Strategy: How to Profit from a World of Big Data, Analytics, and the Internet of Things. Kogan Page, London, UK (2017)

60. Earnshaw R.A.: Interfaces of the Future, Chapter 5 in Research and Development in Digital Media, pp. 63–78. Springer, Cham, Switzerland (2018)

Chapter 5
Geometric Visualization

David Kasik

Abstract While visualization is applicable to any type of data, examining and interacting with geometric data require specialized approaches. Geometric data visualization produces images from a collection of mathematical models, which can be defined interactively or through a set of stored textual commands. Fundamentally, geometric visualization transforms mathematical models into images. Massive model visualization offers interactive performance for visualizing an essentially unlimited amount of geometry. Interactive manipulation assists a person in understanding the nature of an entire 3D model, and allows users to develop models for concept, design, engineering, assembly, and support. The vast majority of devices rely on 2D projections that users must mentally map back into 3D, so a productive interface to the display and the image is a prerequisite for successful design and implementation. Color maps can be used to represent value ranges in order to assist comprehension. Guidelines have been developed from the areas of art and design and applied productively to seeing, drawing, and communicating through geometric and non-geometric images. The earliest solid modeling systems were based on canonical forms that could be assembled through combinatorial solid geometry. Surface representation is important to many application domains because shape can be significant for aerodynamics and aesthetics. Defining and manipulating complex surfaces and shapes have been an area of significant interest throughout the history of Computer-Aided Design and Manufacturing (CAD/CAM). One objective of CAD/CAM is to reap the benefits and cost reductions through design process efficiency. This is particularly important for the automotive and aerospace industries because of the large scale of the products and services that are involved. These industries have pushed the CAD/CAM boundaries in many areas of representation, modeling, and display. Other industry sectors (e.g., shipbuilding, buildings, arts, and entertainment) have benefited from the pioneering work in these areas. This is an illustration of how significant developments in geometric visualization apply across industry domains and the cost/benefits and advantages that accrue to national and international industry. It is also an example of technology transfer, where state-of-the-art research and development has been effectively moved into advanced products and services.

© The Author(s), under exclusive license to Springer Nature Switzerland AG 2019   59
R. Earnshaw et al., *Data Science and Visual Computing*,
SpringerBriefs in Advanced Information and Knowledge Processing,
https://doi.org/10.1007/978-3-030-24367-8_5

Keywords Geometric primitives · Geometry attributes · Computational geometry · 3D models · 3D visualization · Solid modeling · Color maps · Mathematical models · 2D displays · Point representations · Raw geometry · Design process efficiency · Surface patches · Interactive devices · Interactive performance · Aerodynamic characteristics · Computational fluid dynamics · Rendering · Drawing styles · Manufacturing and assembly

5.1   Introduction

This chapter discusses key aspects of geometric visualization: application areas, computational geometry, displays, and creating the illusion of 3D. The objective is to provide context through a brief review of computer graphics and computational geometry history and the effective construction of graphic images to highlight directions for future research.

Ultimately, computer images are specified as a collection of geometric primitives. Fundamentally, a person tells a computer to display points, lines, and polygons, which are geometric forms that represent both geometric and non-geometric content through computer graphics algorithms (Sect. 5.3) on a display (Sect. 5.5). Whether the image represents 2D or 3D content, *geometric visualization* depends on a 2D or 3D mathematical definition (Sect. 5.4). The views selected by a visualization author communicate information about models using a variety of drawing styles and techniques (Sect. 5.6).

Figure 5.1 shows geometric visualization and represents an airport with Boeing 777 aeroplanes.

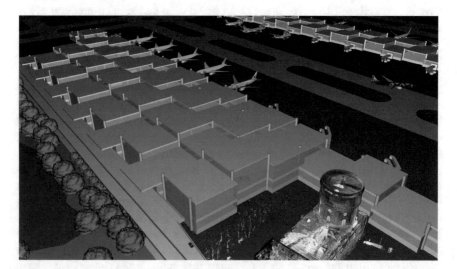

Fig. 5.1 View of airport and Boeing 777s, 9.2 Billion polygons (777 data courtesy of the Boeing Company)

5.2 Geometric Data Input

While there are many disciplines that depend on geometry, geometric data itself are acquired through the following:

- Defining geometric entities (e.g., points, lines, polygons, circles, conic sections, cubes, cylinders, nonuniform rational b-spline surfaces and solids, T-spline surfaces, fractals, subdivision surfaces). The geometric entities can be defined interactively or through a set of stored textual commands. See Sect. 5.4 for a more detailed discussion of computational geometry.
- Digitizing physical objects through scanners, such as ultrasound, computer-aided tomography, or generating content through natural phenomena simulations. The points represent the geometry directly. In some cases, the points are

  - Surface point clouds,
  - volume point clouds (voxels),
  - simply connected with straight lines to form polygons, and
  - input to surface fitting algorithms.

5.3 Geometry-Based Applications

Some application areas rely on geometry that is defined at a higher level than point or voxel clouds. Measurements (such as length, area, and volume) can be derived directly from the geometry.

5.3.1 CAD

Computer-Aided Design (CAD) provided the first substantial application for geometric definition and visualization. Sutherland's 1963 doctoral thesis Sketchpad [1] and GM Research's DAC-1 [2] inspired the industrial CAD movement. CAD was driven by automotive (e.g., GM, Renault, and Ford) and aerospace (e.g., Boeing, Lockheed, McDonnell-Douglas, and British Aerospace) in the 1960s [3, 4]. 2D engineering drawings dominated the field until the early 1990s, when CAD users adopted 3D surfaces and solids more widely. Automotive and aerospace have become totally dependent on 3D CAD geometry. Other industries also deal with designing and building physical structures including home and building construction, shipbuilding, and oil and gas. Each is at a different stage in the extent to which it utilizes CAD. They are gradually approaching automotive and aerospace usage levels to reap the benefits and cost reduction of design process efficiency. Boeing reported greater downstream benefits and cost reductions for the design and production of the 777 [5].

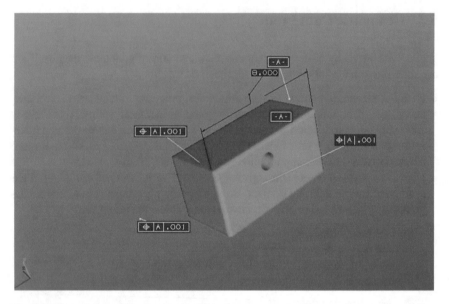

Fig. 5.2   View of basic CAD data (By Kasik, image courtesy of the Boeing Company)

For the purposes of this discussion, CAD represents the use of basic geometric definitions for engineering analysis (CAE), fabrication (part of CAM), assembly (part of CAM), and support (CAS). All industries that depend on CAD have similar visualization needs. Most CAD systems are interactive and viewing the raw geometry is fundamental. Designers define geometry and communicate details using text to instruct manufacturing and assembly users. The resulting annotations can be added to displays of 2D or 3D data and become engineering drawings. Figure 5.2 shows 3D annotations associated with a sample part and product structure.

CAE users often want to examine images that show engineering analysis results mapped onto geometric models. This is often done through color maps that represent value ranges. Color can be used to highlight the degree of stress in the components of structures [6]. This can be computed using finite element analysis.

Assembly, support, and maintenance instruct technicians on the way to perform specific assembly/disassembly. For example, authors often embed geometry as part of initial assembly, disassembly and re-assembly instructions, parts catalogs, and service bulletins. Exploded views of structures can be used in parts catalogs [7].

5.3.2   Animation

The field of computer animation started around the same time as CAD. While some CAD geometry found its way into animated films, specialized geometry definition systems (e.g., SynthaVision, Maya) were developed. These systems could relax geometric precision because only "virtual" images were needed. Computer animation grew enormously when the entertainment industry started developing special effects economically in the mid1990s.

While CAD demands interactive performance throughout, animation needs interactive visualization rates during geometry definition, scene setup (e.g., lighting and rigging), and review. The final animation sequences result from batch processing in which each frame is computed for viewing. Even so, the fundamental geometric entities are the same: points, lines, polygons, surfaces, and solids. The differentiator is in the set of geometry attributes that govern the display. CAD geometry often requires greater definitional accuracy because physical parts are built from the geometry.

5.3.3 Electronic Games

Interactive, graphics-based electronic games have existed since computer operator consoles supported line drawings. Since the consoles were almost always in locked rooms, operators were the primary players. The basic geometry in today's games is similar to CAD and animation. The differentiator is interactive performance. Game developers seek to keep players playing for longer and longer periods. Since 3D scenes dominate the games market, rendering rates are maintained at rates that exceed 60 Hz. Game developers seek to reduce scene complexity by decreasing polygon count, using texture mapping, dropping polygons, and other scene simplification techniques.

5.3.4 Point-Based Applications

Any geometry-based system can ultimately generate points or voxels. The applications defined in this section are based on points or voxels as raw input. Surfaces and solids can be derived from the points and voxels. Most often, the visualization applications use the points and voxels directly.

Raw data are generally acquired from a digitizing device, such as in medicine (for example, X-ray, ultrasound, and computer-assisted tomography), reverse engineering (from 3D scanners), map display (from cameras), and motion (from multiple cameras) are examples.

Scientific visualization [8] adds point representations derived from simulation of natural phenomena. Since the raw data are based only on points, specialized display algorithms are used for both interactive applications and animations. Scientific visualization needs the same performance levels as CAD for its interactive visualization systems. The results of analysis (see Fig. 5.3) may need millions of points to show the level of detail required.

The featured image displays plots of a CGNS dataset representing a YF-17 jet aircraft. The dataset consists of an unstructured grid with solution. VisIt created the

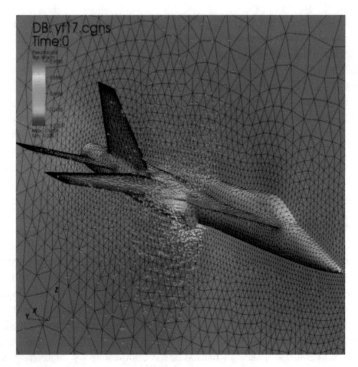

Fig. 5.3 Mach/vector plot of YF-17. Public domain image—https://en.wikipedia.org/wiki/Scientific_visualization#/media/File:YF-17_aircraft_Plot.jpg

image using a Pseudocolor plot of the dataset's Mach variable, a Mesh plot of the grid, and Vector plot of a slice through the Velocity field.

5.4   Computational Geometry

Point, line, and polygon coordinates are specified as (x, y) or (x, y, z) coordinates in Euclidean space and are independent of display type. Standard transformations convert from alternate coordinate systems (e.g., polar, spherical, and cylindrical). Each geometric primitive has a set of attributes that controls its appearance. The attributes include visibility, color, texture, and pattern. More complex geometric forms must be converted into points, lines, and polygons for rendering. For example, graphics algorithms convert circles into short, connected line segments and surfaces into three- or four-sided polygons.

An introduction and general overview of computational geometry is provided by Preparata and Shamos [9]. This section briefly examines the methods and techniques used for computational geometry to support CAD in automotive, CAD in aerospace, and animation/games. Point-based applications dominate scientific visualization. Since they are point based and may need to represent more complex surfaces for additional analysis and high-accuracy rendering, scientific visualization practitioners may employ surface fitting applications.

Mathematics is an ancient field and can trace its roots to prehistory [10]. The Sumerians, Egyptians, and Greeks all made significant contributions. While not specifically attributable, the Egyptians must have had a basic understanding of geometry to design and build the pyramids. As noted in Sect. 5.3.1, early CAD systems [1, 3] focused on 2D engineering drawings. The fundamental shapes were based on equations for the canonical forms common in analytical geometry. Research into 3D representations, both surface and solid, started in the late 1960s and 1970s. The remainder of this section gives examples of early systems. The computational geometry systems in use today are largely based on the mathematics developed and gradually improved over the past 50 years.

5.4.1 Solid Modeling

The earliest solid modeling systems were based on canonical forms that could be assembled through Constructive Solid Geometry (CSG). Systems developed in the late 1970s and 1980s generalized solid modeling and moved from primitive shapes to Boundary-representations (B-rep) of both primitive and surface-bounded shapes. Shape Data [11] based its Romulus software on solid primitives. Romulus evolved into Parasolid [12], a full B-rep system, in the 1990s. The Mathematics Applications Group (MAGI) started development of the Synthavision system in the early 1970s [13]. MAGI used CSG techniques with primitive shapes only to develop scenes with trees, roads, and camouflage. It produced a significant amount of the computer animation for the first Tron feature film [14].

Figure 5.4 shows a boundary representation-defined solid model. B-rep systems use the same Boolean operations to combine primitives (union, intersection) and create holes (subtraction). Today's dominant CAD systems are based on B-rep solids.

5.4.2 Automotive Body Surfaces

In addition to improving the development and maintenance of engineering drawings, the automotive industry pushed the boundaries of surfaces representing automobile bodies. Bill Gordon (General Motors), Pierre Bezier (Renault), Steve Coons (MIT), and Albert Overhauser (Ford) formulated early surface patch definitions. In addition to direct representation, the patches had to be adaptable to fit a collection of points digitized directly from clay models [15].

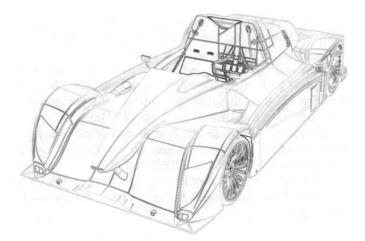

Fig. 5.4 Automobile defined by B-rep solids (Coachwork example, public domain image—https://en.wikipedia.org/wiki/Boundary_representation#/media/File:WEAZER0.jpg)

5.4.3   Aerospace Control Surfaces

Both aerospace and automotive industries have strong interest in aerodynamic characteristics. The overall aerospace design process differs from automotive because of product scale. The automotive industry is also concerned about showroom lighting effects. Aerospace has designed complex surfaces since the early 1900s that are encapsulated in handbooks (see Fig. 5.5). The digital models are used to produce both physical wind-tunnel test models and digital input to computational fluid dynamic software.

Many of the NACA shapes are based on conics and conic sections. As the CAD industry investigated generalized forms to produce more complex curves and sur-

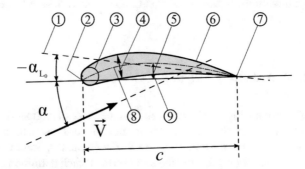

Fig. 5.5 Sample NACA airfoil (Released into the public domain by Flanker, https://commons.wikimedia.org/wiki/File:Airfoil_geometry.svg). Profile geometry—1: Zero lift line; 2: Leading edge; 3: Nose circle; 4: Max. thickness; 5: Camber; 6: Upper surface; 7: Trailing edge; 8: Camber mean-line; 9: Lower surface

faces that could be represented by analytical forms, Boeing researchers [16] settled on Nonuniform Rational B-splines (NURBS) [17]. Unlike polynomials and other spline forms, NURBS curves and surfaces can represent conic sections with a single definition. CAD systems developed in the 1980s and 1990s added NURBS-bounded surfaces to solids in systems like Parasolid (the successor to Shape Data Limited's software [12]) and ACIS [18].

While NURBS still dominate the CAD industry, other spline forms (e.g., T-splines, Catmull–Rom splines, rational B-splines, and cardinal) have found their way into some systems. CAD systems often provide a user interface based on mathematical forms simpler than NURBS and store NURBS internally.

5.4.4 Animation and Games

Outside the transportation and building industries, requirements for surface accuracy are less stringent. This has led to a number of surfaces that automatically add shape detail or represent natural phenomena. Examples include subdivision surfaces, fractals, blobs, trees, water, and many others.

Figure 5.6 shows how surface approximations can be more accurate (and therefore more realistic) using quadric error metrics. The control is provided through subdivision surfaces that are refined under mathematical control as the magnification level increases [19].

In contrast to subdivision surfaces, fractals add detail to complex scenes through a controlled stochastic method as the zoom level increases [20–22]. As a result, fractals are frequently used to represent synthetic landscapes. Early work shown at the 1980 SIGGRAPH conference included a fractal landscape film Vol Libre [23] by Carpenter [24] and landscape images [25]. Figure 5.7 shows an example of a synthetic, fractal-generated landscape.

Fig. 5.6 Successive approximations of a surface computed using quadric error metrics applied to the "Stanford bunny". Public domain, https://commons.wikimedia.org/w/index.php?curid=24638787, https://upload.wikimedia.org/wikipedia/commons/1/1b/Stanford_bunny_qem.png

Fig. 5.7 Fractal landscape, an example of computer-generated imagery (by The Ostrich—Own work, CC BY 3.0, https://commons.wikimedia.org/w/index.php?curid=4716597), https://upload.wikimedia.org/wikipedia/commons/6/6e/FractalLandscape.jpg

Blobby models are based on implicit surfaces. Many consider Blinn [26] as the first to publish and use blobs. His application was molecular models, and blobs have been used extensively since.

5.4.5 Fitting

As noted in Sect. 5.2, points represent the simplest geometric form. Computational geometry algorithms fit collections of points to curves and surfaces. The resulting curves and surfaces are then used as input to downstream applications. Surface fitting algorithms must often process hundreds and thousands of points.

5.5 Communication Impact

The overall intent of geometric visualization is to communicate. Ultimately, a computer generates an image from a raw 3D geometric definition. The image should be able to improve a viewer's understanding or appreciation. Sometimes, view authors (e.g., artists) are trying to make a point. Others (e.g., design engineers) want to help the viewer understand context, design intent, manufacturability, and supportability.

There is a rich field in the psychology of visualization that describes why certain visual cues can let people infer 3D on a flat screen. Peddie [27] traces the evolution of specific techniques to prehistoric times. Massironi [28] and many others credit Leonardo da Vinci with developing a systematic approach to perspective. Other types of projections assist in understanding an image. Coordinate transformations (cylindrical, spherical) can improve understanding, especially for scientific visualization. Specialized map projections [29] are especially useful when showing cartographic data.

In actual practice, the viewer must assess the meaning of the overall image. The image author is responsible for telling a story; the viewer consumes it. Viewers can infer meaning even if the pictures have problems. For example, vision scientists have looked at how

- Pictures can lie by misrepresenting data whether accidentally or deliberately.
- Humans can have change blindness [30].
- Humans can infer meaning even with deliberate misspellings [31].
- Humans can be trained to detect subtle, seemingly undetectable cues [32].

Massironi studied art and art history and derived not only an effective taxonomy of image styles but also a set basic visual cues and the information they communicate [28]. He stresses the importance of establishing context, creating drawing components that highlight content, perspective to show 3D, non-photorealistic techniques, and text annotations to reduce ambiguity. Essentially, the book provides an excellent guide to the individual elements of a single picture and what each element adds. Massironi developed guidelines that improve an image author's ability to communicate his/her message. The guidelines apply to any style of art, whether representing a geometric subject or something totally abstract. Since the guidelines are derived from art over the centuries, they have clear empirical justification. Stevens describes naturally occurring patterns, another method of generating visual cues with which we are familiar and comfortable [33]. Massironi's guidelines apply to seeing, drawing, and communicating information through the initial display of geometric and non-geometric images. Computers give a viewer more latitude to dynamically change

- Orientation through interactive image manipulation.
- Stereo viewing.
- Rendering style.

There is little research on how giving a user such image modification flexibility affects a person's ability to understand geometric images. The field of information visualization seeks to construct images that communicate ab initio. Initial images benefit from Massironi's fundamentals and many others (e.g., Jacques Bertin, Colin Ware, and Edward Tufte). Visual analytics adds interaction to help confirm the expected and detect the unexpected. Some visual analytics papers evaluate application usability, not communication impact based on dynamic change. Geometric visualization has stressed task performance [34, 35] rather than communication impact.

5.6 Conclusions

Many industries have been able to use these developments in geometry and modeling. All continue to benefit from the efficiency and effectiveness of computer-aided design processes. There have been further advances that provide "virtual walk-throughs" of geometric designs. Sophisticated 3D walk-throughs apply to multiple industries and are generally industry independent. They allow complex design exploration and design error detection (e.g., incorrect gaps and unexpected collisions). Moreover, others outside design use walk-throughs to assess manufacturability, supportability, ergonomics, design integration, and other tasks. In short, use of geometric designs across the product lifecycle offers extraordinary benefits.

The ability to use computer-generated images offers geometry viewers new possibilities. Given the extensive use of 2D and 3D geometry as the definitional basis for many fields, both authors and viewers have increased choice in creating initial geometry views and changing them dynamically. The geometry visualization community continues to push the boundaries by adding new devices and rendering methods. The work has resulted in increasingly realistic images with even more parameters to control. The complexity of interaction with visual images has been assisted by the formulation of guidelines to seeing, drawing, and communicating information in the display of both geometric and non-geometric data. The technology to combine multiple physical display types with the convenience and speed of defining rendering styles offers new opportunities to improve geometry visualization. Correlating the technology with specific tasks to choose the most effective initial display and visualization toolsets can make geometry visualization even more effective than it is today.

Further Reading

Catmull, E. and Wallace, A. Creativity, Inc.: Overcoming the Unseen Forces That Stand in the Way of True Inspiration. Transworld Publishers, London, UK (2014), ISBN-13 978-0812993011

Goldman, R. An Integrated Introduction to Computer Graphics and Geometric Modeling. CRC Press Taylor and Francis Group, Boca Raton, FL (2009), ISBN-13: 978-1439803349

Golovanov, N. Geometric Modeling: The mathematics of shapes, Academia Publishing House (2014). ISBN-13 978-1497473195

Mortenson, M. E. Geometric Modeling. Third Edition, Wiley Computer Publishing, Hoboken, NJ (2006). ISBN-13: 978-0831132989

Tufte, E. The Visual Display of Quantitative Information 2nd Edition. Graphics Press, Cheshire, CT (2001), ISBN-13: 978-0961392147

Wilkinson, L., Wills, D., Rope, D., Norton, A., Dubbs, R. The Grammar of Graphics (Statistics and Computing) Second Edition. Springer, New York, NY (2006), ISBN-13: 978-0387245447.

References

1. Sutherland, I.E.: Sketchpad: A Man-Machine Graphical Communication System. MIT, Cambridge, MA (1963, 2003). https://www.cl.cam.ac.uk/techreports/UCAM-CL-TR-574.pdf
2. Krull, F.N.: The origin of computer graphics within General Motors. IEEE Ann. Hist. Comput. **16** (3), 40–56 (1994) (IEEE, New York, NY). https://dl.acm.org/citation.cfm?id=612564
3. Weisberg, D.E.: The Engineering Design Revolution (2008). http://www.cadhistory.net/
4. Dill, J., Kasik, D.: Discovering and transitioning technology, Chapter 27. In: Expanding the Frontiers of Visual Analytics and Visualization. Springer, Cham, Switzerland (2012). https://www.springer.com/us/book/9781447128038
5. ICMRIndia: The Making of the 777. http://www.icmrindia.org/casestudies/catalogue/Operations/Making%20of%20Boeing%20777-Operations%20Management%20Case%20Studies.htm
6. http://www.fracturemechanics.org/hole.html
7. https://www.poolzoom.com/polaris-360-replacement-pool-cleaner-parts.html
8. https://en.wikipedia.org/wiki/Scientific_visualization
9. Preparata, F.P., Shamos, M.I.: Computational Geometry: An Introduction, 1st edn. Springer, New York, NY (1985). ISBN 0-387-96131-3 (5th printing, corrected and expanded, 1993)
10. Mastin, L.: The Story of Mathematics (2010). https://www.storyofmathematics.com/, https://www.storyofmathematics.com/story.html
11. https://en.wikipedia.org/wiki/Shape_Data_Limited
12. https://en.wikipedia.org/wiki/Parasolid
13. https://en.wikipedia.org/wiki/Mathematical_Applications_Group
14. https://en.wikipedia.org/wiki/Tron
15. http://www.bbc.com/autos/story/20161111-why-car-designers-stick-with-clay
16. Blomgren, R.M., Kasik, D.J.: Early investigation, formulation, and use of NURBS at Boeing. ACM SIGGRAPH Comput. Graph. **36**(3), 27–32 (2002) (ACM, New York, NY). https://dl.acm.org/citation.cfm?id=570345
17. de Boor, C.: A Practical Guide to Splines. Springer, New York, NY (2001)
18. https://en.wikipedia.org/wiki/ACIS
19. Lee, A., Moreton, H., Hoppe, H.: Displaced subdivision surfaces. In: ACM SIGGRAPH Computer Graphics, vol. 27 Special Issue, Proceedings of the 27th Annual Conference on Computer Graphics and Interactive Techniques, pp 85–94. ACM, New York, NY (2000). https://dl.acm.org/citation.cfm?doid=344779.344829, http://hhoppe.com/dss.pdf
20. Mandelbrot, B.: The Fractal Geometry of Nature. W.H. Freeman & Co Ltd., London, UK (1982)
21. Crilly, A.J., Earnshaw, R.A., Jones, H. (eds.): Fractals and Chaos. Springer, New York, NY (1991)
22. Falconer, K.: Fractals: A Very Short Introduction. Oxford University Press, Oxford, UK (2013)
23. https://kottke.org/09/07/vol-libre-an-amazing-cg-film-from-1980 (includes the online video)
24. Carpenter, L.: Computer rendering of fractal curves and surfaces. In: ACM SIGGRAPH Computer Graphics, vol. 14, Special Issue. ACM, New York, NY (1980). http://old.siggraph.org/publications/rarities/carpenter-1980supp.pdf
25. Fournier, A., Fussell, D.: Stochastic modeling in computer graphics. In: ACM SIGGRAPH Computer Graphics, vol. 14, Special Issue, pp. 1–8. ACM, New York, NY (1980). http://old.siggraph.org/publications/rarities/fournier-fussell-1980supp.pdf
26. Blinn, J.F.: A generalization of algebraic surface drawing. ACM Trans. Graph. **1**(3), 235–256 (1982) (ACM, New York, NY). https://dl.acm.org/citation.cfm?id=357306.357310
27. Peddie, J.: The History of Visual Magic in Computers: How Beautiful Images are Made in CAD, 3D, VR and AR. Springer, London (2013)
28. Massironi, M.: The Psychology of Graphic Images: Seeing, Drawing, Communicating. Psychology Press, Hove, UK (2001)
29. https://en.wikipedia.org/wiki/Map_projection

30. Rensink, R.: Change blindness. In: Itti, L., Rees, G., Tsotsos, J.K. (eds.) Neurobiology of Attention, pp. 76–81. Academic Press, San Diego, CA (2005). https://philpapers.org/rec/ITTNOA

31. Rayner, K., White, S.J. Johnson, R.L., Liversedge, S.P.: Raeding wrods with jubmled lettres: there is a cost. Psychol. Sci. **17**(3), 92–193 (2006). https://www.ncbi.nlm.nih.gov/pubmed/16507057

32. Biederman, I., Shiffrar, M.M.: Sexing day-old chicks: a case study and expert systems analysis of a difficult perceptual-learning task. J. Exp. Psychol. Learn. Mem. Cogn. **13**(4), 640–645 (1987). http://dx.doi.org/10.1037/0278-7393.13.4.640

33. Stevens, P.S.: Patterns in Nature. Little Brown & Co., New York, NY (1979)

34. Kasik, D.J., Troy, J.J., Amorosi, S.R., Murray, M.O., Swamy, S.N.: Evaluating graphics displays for complex 3D models. IEEE Comput. Graph. Appl. **22**(3), 56–64 (2002) (IEEE). https://doi.org/10.1109/mcg.2002.999788

35. Swindells, C., Po, B.A., Hajshirmohammadi, I., Corrie, B., Dill, J.C., Fisher, B.D., Booth, K.S.: Comparing CAVE, wall, and desktop displays for navigation and wayfinding in complex 3D models. In: Proceedings of Computer Graphics International Conference, 420–427, (2004). https://www.researchgate.net/publication/232656533/download, https://ieeexplore.ieee.org/document/1309243

Chapter 6
Visual Analytics

Rae Earnshaw

Abstract An overview of the history, development, and applications of visual analytics is provided. Readers familiar with some of the research and development aspects in visual analytics should also benefit from this review of the field's genesis and objectives. The principal drivers for the generation of the field are summarized and the initial research and development agenda that followed from these is reviewed. The distinctive aspects of visual analytics are discussed in relation to other forms of visualization. A wide variety of software for visual analytics is summarized and a methodology for effective comparison is proposed. The current trend toward large collaborative research and development projects across institutions and organizations, and between the academy and industry, is analyzed and reviewed in the context of visualization research. A number of typical applications in interactive data visualization are presented, while recognizing the limitations of presenting these solely in a written and visual format when their power is normally in real-time interactive exploration. Aspects of current research and development in visual analytics are presented and compared with those in scientific visualization and information visualization. The question of whether visual analytics has subsumed the areas of information visualization and scientific visualization is considered. Possible future directions for visual analytics are explored.

Keywords Visual communication · Visual representation · Human cognition · Cognitive processing · User-centered evaluation · Human perception · Analytical reasoning · Time-critical data analysis · Knowledge generation · Machine learning · Data streaming · Autonomous analytics · Big data analytics · Extreme-scale data · Collaborative research and development · Storytelling · Theoretical foundations

6.1   Introduction

Major initiatives often have specific drivers and circumstances which bring them into being and which provide the focus for investigation and analysis, and also subsequent applications which build on these developments. The Scientific Revolution in the fifteenth and sixteenth centuries was one such development and it was initiated in part by a new and systematic view of the natural world defined by Newton [1] which operated by fixed laws which could be represented by mathematics, and partly by the availability of resources for experimentation and the development of the natural sciences.

The driver for the first stored-program digital computer in 1946 was, according to its name ENIAC, USA [2] and EDSAC, UK [3], able to perform numerical calculations much faster than by the earlier mechanical means. Bowden [4] captured the key attribute of this new invention—it could calculate much faster than a human could think. Valves (vacuum tubes) gave way to transistors and the rest is history. Both the Scientific Revolution and the advent of the digital computer may be considered paradigm shifts according to the definition advanced by Kuhn [5].

The driver for Scientific Visualization, as discussed earlier, was the requirement of the *National Science Foundation's Division of Advanced Scientific Computing in the USA in 1987 for advice on how best to utilize supercomputers to meet users' needs in a variety of scientific disciplines. Many of these were producing "fire-hoses" of data that far outstripped the computational capability to analyze them even with supercomputers. The report, Visualization in Scientific Computing* (McCormick et al. [6]), *was produced after consultation and described how such an initiative could be accomplished, and has provided the basis for much of the subsequent development in this field.*

In a similar way, the driver for the development of visual analytics was the requirement of the US Department of Homeland of Security in 2004 to have better IT tools and facilities (Hennessy et al. [7]) *for the protection of its national and international borders. Much data were already available in different forms and different places but it was also massive, complex, incomplete, dynamic, and uncertain. Networks could integrate databases, but facilities were needed to provide the best analyses of the data, which was often varying in real time. It was therefore requested that the National Visualization and Analytics Centre (NVAC)* [8] *to define a research and development agenda to facilitate advanced analytical insight. After international consultation and two working group meetings, the report:* Illuminating the Path: The Research and Development Agenda for Visual Analytics (Thomas and Cook [9]) was produced. This report included the following key areas:

- The science of analytical reasoning.
- Visual representations and interaction techniques.
- Data representations and transformations.
- Production, presentation, and dissemination of actionable information to decision-makers in a form understandable by them.
- Moving research into practice.

Each of these areas produced a number of recommendations for the further work, or action, that was needed.

Prerequisites of the initial requirements implicitly included

- *The ability to aggregate heterogeneous datasets.*
- *The need to be able to interact effectively with the data.*
- *Efficient and effective visualizations that could link into the human cognitive processes.*
- *Incorporation of real-time data, whether autonomous or from direct human input.*
- *Incorporation of portable, handheld, devices for mobile analytics.*

The McKenzie Report (Henke et al. [10]) *detailed the ways in which visual analytics is able to address the challenges of a data-driven world.* Fisher et al. [11] *and* Hong et al. [12] *reviewed aspects of the visual analytics for big data.*

6.2 Defining Visual Analytics

According to Thomas and Cook (2005), visual analytics may be defined as follows:

> *the science of analytical reasoning facilitated by interactive visual interfaces. People use visual analytics tools and techniques to synthesize information and derive insight from massive, dynamic, ambiguous, and often conflicting data; detect the expected and discover the unexpected; provide timely, defensible, and understandable assessments; and communicate assessment effectively for action*

> *Visual analytics is a multidisciplinary field that includes the following focus areas:*

> - **Analytical reasoning techniques** *that enable users to obtain deep insights that directly support assessment, planning, and decision making*
> - **Visual representations and interaction techniques** *that take advantage of the human eye's broad bandwidth pathway into the mind to allow users to see, explore, and understand large amounts of information at once*
> - **Data representations and transformations** *that convert all types of conflicting and dynamic data in ways that support visualization and analysis*
> - *Techniques to support* **production, presentation, and dissemination** *of the results of an analysis to communicate information in the appropriate context to a variety of audiences*

Visual analytics therefore represents a development "*of the fields of information visualization and scientific visualization that focuses on analytical reasoning facilitated by interactive visual interfaces*" [13]. This close coupling of the human reasoning, cognitive ability, and computer processing and display make visual analytics suitable for large and complex problems which could be more difficult to address by other methods. It has therefore been closely associated with the analysis of big data.

This may be summarized as follows:

- *Scientific visualization deals with data that has a natural geometric structure (e.g., MRI data, wind flows).*
- *Information visualization handles abstract data structures such as trees or graphs.*
- *Visual analytics is especially concerned with coupling interactive visual representations with underlying analytical processes (e.g., statistical procedures, data mining techniques) such that high-level, complex activities can be effectively performed (e.g., sense making, reasoning, presentation, decision making)* [13].

Keim et al. [14] formulated a visual analytics "mantra" to capture the overall process of the VA method: analyze first, show the important, zoom, filter, and analyze further details on demand.

A key component of visual analytics, therefore, is the potential to magnify and augment human cognitive power and capability by means of:

- *increasing cognitive resources, such as by using a visual resource to expand human working memory,*
- *reducing search, such as by representing a large amount of data in a small space,*
- *enhancing the recognition of patterns, such as when information is organized in space by its time relationships,*
- *supporting the easy perceptual inference of relationships that are otherwise more difficult to induce,*
- *perceptual monitoring of a large number of potential events, and*
- *providing a manipulable medium that, unlike static diagrams, enables the exploration of a space of parameter values* [9].

Scholtz et al. [15] provide an introduction to visual analytics.

6.3 What Makes Visual Analytics Distinctive?

A possible objection to the foregoing analysis is to say that humans can be unreliable in performing specific tasks, and therefore can be unreliable at interacting with data. It would be safer to allow the computer to perform the numerical calculations and output the results, which could then be acted on by the human. In other words, keeping the human out of the loop could be a more preferable option. This is certainly true for computing tasks which are generally automated, e.g., checking credit card information for a transaction at a point-of-sale device against a database of valid cards. In this case, there is only one of two possible results: valid or invalid. Thus, in simple cases, when the information is numerical and quantitative, the analysis can be performed by the computer alone. However, often the data that are available are representing a situation about which there is some uncertainty. The computer analysis will have little knowledge or information about this external uncertainty, and therefore human guidance on which part, or parts, of the data to analyze is needed. In addition, if there is some time-critical element required in the analysis, then human intervention may be mandatory. An example of this is the decisions to be made at frontier posts on whether to let particular cargos pass through, or whether they should be stopped and searched. The computer may have information about the company's products and services in its database along with its trading records and any previous customs infringements, but may be unlikely to have specific information on this particular movement of goods. The human observer at the border will have additional local information, and may also have sensor data from devices used to detect illegal substances. The combination of these two sets of information is crucial to making a decision about what to do next. Clearly, such time-critical decisions also need to be optimal and as accurate as possible. Searching more trucks and vehicles than is necessary could lead to long traffic delays and adverse economic effects. In this case, keeping the human in the loop is key to the success of the overall evaluation and the efficiency of the process. An advantage to this approach is the judgement that the human can exercise based on their evaluation of the overall situation and their experience of similar incidents in the past that they can draw on. A possible disadvantage to the human in the loop is human error in inputting data from the particular local situation. One solution to this is to have automated sensor and vision data input, but human judgement may still be required on the overall analysis in order to reach an optimum decision.

This coupling of human reasoning and experience with computational analysis is the principal strength of visual analytics. This implies that the relationship between these two components needs to be fully understood, and numerous research projects are seeking to explore this area in greater detail. In addition, the cognitive processes involved in human reasoning are the subject of ongoing research in order to get a better understanding of how humans process key information. Finally, the kind of visual representations appropriate to accurate and efficient decision-making is also being explored in more detail. For example, a visualization that is chosen for a scientific analysis of a simulation may not be appropriate for a security application where there is real-time data being analyzed.

Visual analytics may be expressed diagrammatically as shown in Fig. 6.1.

Keim et al. [16] outline the challenges associated with analyzing large amounts of data. Yang and Wu [17] detail ten challenges associated with data mining research. Järvinen et al. [18] present the findings of a project by VTT, TKK, and Helsinki Institute of Information Technology on the concept of visual analytics and the state of visual analytics research and development, and its relevance for industrial and consumer applications in Finland.

6.4 Software for Visual Analytics

Following on from an earlier survey of commercial systems by Zhang et al. [19], a further analysis was performed by Behrisch et al. in 2018 [20]. Evaluation was based on a number of aspects including features, performance, usability, suitability for specific user groups, and ability to handle complex data types. Possible future

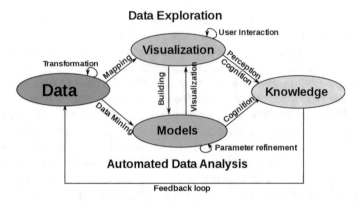

Fig. 6.1 The visual analytics workflow. Based on D. A. Keim, J. Kohlhammer, G. P. Ellis, F. Mansmann: Mastering The Information Age—Solving Problems with Visual Analytics. Eurographics, 2010. Licensed under the Creative Commons Attribution-Share Alike 4.0 International license (https://commons.wikimedia.org/wiki/File:VisualAnalyticsWorkflow.svg)

developments are also proposed. This followed on from the earlier survey [19] and therefore developments in the software over this period were noted, including the entry of new products into the market place. The visual analytics market is estimated to be worth $6.5 billion by 2022 [21] (from $2.2 billion in 2016) and it is therefore a highly competitive area with many companies seeking to capitalize on the opportunities presented by the increasing volumes of data, and the increasing adoption by the market place of visual analytics tools. A number of software and systems providers are seeking to augment their analytics products with the power of Artificial Intelligence (AI) in order to provide enhanced capability and to increase their leverage in the market place.

Scholtz [22] emphasizes the importance of including the user and their intended application(s) in the evaluation of visual analytics software, and not just comparing the functions within the software available, or their interfaces. There may be some specific difficulties with the data in the particular application area, and therefore a good match is needed between the analytics software and the application. In other words, there can be gap between the design of a visual analytics tool and its use in actual practice. User-centered evaluations of analytics software are essential in order to obtain an accurate view of their applicability to the domain of interest. Aspects of the user's requirements include the tasks to be performed, the data (and metadata) to be used, the filtering processes to be applied to the data, and the thinking processes that the users engage in when seeking to understand the meaning of the data. For example, for the latter aspect, it may take time for a user to understand the significance of a visualization when it changes. The cognitive processes of the human are often overlooked in the analysis of data and the operation of the visual analytics software. Such user-centered evaluations may become even more important as new functions (such as AI) are added to future software. Scholtz [22] also includes visual analytics case studies adapted from the intelligence and human–computer interaction communities to illustrate the principles advanced.

Table 6.1 shows examples of visual analytics software.

According to Behrisch et al. [20], QlikView, Spotfire, PowerBI, and Tableau are the established key players in the field. A number of the products listed in Table 6.1 offer free downloads of older versions, or versions with reduced functionality, in order to give potential users an opportunity to access and use the software on their data. Harger and Crossno [23] reviewed open-source visual analytics toolkits that were available in 2012. Although this has largely been superseded by commercial companies offering free downloads, the methodology employed to compare the toolkits is still useful to consider, alongside the importance of a user-centered evaluation as detailed by Scholtz [22].

6.5 National Visualization and Analytics Centers

6.5.1 Collaborative Research and Development

The current trend toward large research projects is exemplified by funding programs in the UK, the European Union, and the National Science Foundation (NSF). In the UK, the larger projects involve inter-institution collaborations where the combined research strength is believed to be greater than the sum of the parts [24]. In addition, collaboration is often required when interdisciplinary research is involved. In the European Union, many research and development projects involve collaborations between institutions and organizations across at least three European countries and usually involve industrial partners, especially where the outputs of the projects are expected to be new products or services.

In the USA, 24 National Science Foundation Science and Technology Centers were created in 1987 to pursue foundational interdisciplinary research. The objective was to address increasing global competition, and to develop innovative, interdisciplinary approaches in important areas of basic research. The first STCs were established in 1989 and more were added in 1991. The STC Program was administered through the Office of Science and Technology Infrastructure at NSF. Examples were

- Centers in the Biological Sciences (BIO).
- Centers in Computer and Information Science and Engineering (CISE).
- Centers in the Geosciences (GEO).
- Centers in the Mathematical and Physical Sciences (MPS).
- Centers in Social, Behavioral and Economic Sciences (SBE).

A Graphics and Visualization Centre [25] was established in 1991 which was a consortium of research groups from five universities: Brown University, the California Institute of Technology (Caltech), Cornell University, the University of North Car-

Table 6.1 Examples of visual analytics software

Software	Developer	Key functions	Date/Employees	Website, revenue
Tableau	Tableau Software/from Stanford University	Interactive data visualization products focused on business intelligence	3,500 (2017) Acquired an AI startup, Empirical Systems, in June 2018	https://www.tableau.com/ $877 m (2017)
QlikView	Qlik Technologies	Data discoveries	2,500 (2015), founded 1993, Lund, Sweden	https://www.qlik.com/en-gb/products/qlikview
Spotfire	Tibco/from University of Maryland	Visual data analysis tool	190	https://spotfire.tibco.com/
PowerBI	Microsoft	Data mining, business intelligence	2013	http://powerbi.microsoft.com/en-us/
Advizor	Advizor Solutions	Interactive data visualization		https://www.advizorsolutions.com/
Cognos	IBM	Business analytics, web-based integrated business intelligence suite	3,500 (2007)	https://www.ibm.com/products/cognos-analytics $980 m (2007)
JMP	SAS	Statistical analysis		https://www.jmp.com/en_gb/home.html
Visual Analytics	SAS	Graphical user interface that can be used to visually explore and report SAS data		https://www.sas.com/en_gb/software/visual-analytics.html
JasperSoft	Tibco	Business intelligence		https://www.jaspersoft.com/
SAP Lumira	SAP	Business intelligence		https://saplumira.com/
Geotime	Uncharted Software Inc	Visual analysis of events over time	2005	http://geotime.com

(continued)

Table 6.1 (continued)

Software	Developer	Key functions	Date/Employees	Website, revenue
Qlik Sense	Qlik Sense	Explore simple and complex data to find the hidden data relationships	2,500 (2015), founded 1993, Lund, Sweden	http://www.qlik.com/us/products/qlik-sense
Inspire	Pacific Northwest National Laboratory	Visual document analysis	1995 Several thousand employees	http://in-spire.pnml.gov/
FusionCharts	FusionCharts	JavaScript-based charting and visualization package It can produce 90 different chart types and integrates with a large number of platforms and frameworks giving a great deal of flexibility	Not known	http://www.fusioncharts.com/
Highcharts	Highcharts	Cross-browser, interactive visualization	Not known	https://www.highcharts.com/
Datawrapper	Datawrapper	Charts and statistics	Not known	https://www.datawrapper.de/
Plotly	Plotly	Integration with analytics-oriented programming languages such as Python, R, and MATLAB	2013, 37 employees https://craft.co/plotly	https://plot.ly/
Sisense	Sisense	Multiple sources of data	Not known	https://www.sisense.com/
Geotime	Uncharted	Patterns in time and space	Early 2000s	https://uncharted.software/

Some of the data in Table 6.1 is courtesy of—https://www.forbes.com/sites/bernardmarr/2017/07/20/the-7-best-data-visualization-tools-in-2017/#2c5d89976c30 olina at Chapel Hill, and the University of Utah. It conducted research in modeling, rendering, high-performance architectures, graphical interaction and communication, and scientific visualization.

6.5.2   USA—National Visualization and Analytics Centers

In order to implement the research and development agenda defined by Thomas and Cook [9], the Department of Homeland Security set up a network of Visualization and Analytics Centers [26] to advance the various functional areas. This network included University of Washington, Stanford University, Purdue University, Pennsylvania State University, Georgia Institute of Technology, and University of North Carolina at Charlotte [27].

Areas of interest to the network of Visualization and Analytics Centers included

- Data wrangling and preparation,
- Distributed storage architectures,
- Advanced computational concepts,
- Analytics and visualization,
- Human-centered systems,
- Decision support and business processes,
- Privacy and security, and
- Analytics for the Internet of Things and embedded systems.

A Visualization Center for Command Control and Interoperability Environments (VACCINE) [28] is centered on Purdue University and created methods, tools, and applications to analyze and manage the large amounts of information for all mission areas of homeland security in the most efficient manner. It was established as a Center of Excellence by the Department of Homeland Security Science and Technology Directorate.

6.5.3   Canadian Network for Visual Analytics

In Canada, a related network for visual analytics (CANVAC) [29] was set up in Vancouver in 2012 to:

> address the needs of a growing visual analytics (VA) research community in Canada by supporting the requirements of all VA stakeholders, i.e., researchers, developers and user organizations. CANVAC has the following goals:
>
> - To develop and assist in the development of visual analytics expertise in Canada.
> - To facilitate and promote research conducted in the field of visual analytics.
> - To support and promote education and training in visual analytics in academia and industry.

- *To promote and represent the Canadian visual analytics community internationally* [29].

The founding members included the University of British Columbia, Simon Fraser University, and Dalhousie University, and further participants included University of Alberta, University of Calgary, York University, OCAD University, and University of New Brunswick. Industry partners included those involved in utilizing visual analytics tools, and also companies involved in aerospace, safety and security, health care, telecommunications, and transportation. Links are also maintained with NVAC in the United States, UKVAC in England, BRAVA in Brazil, and VisMaster in the EU.

CANVAC focussed on visual analytics techniques to

- Acquire and manage large amounts of data.
- Visually explore and synthesize information.
- Derive insight from massive, dynamic, ambiguous, and often conflicting data.
- Provide assessments that are timely, defensible, and understandable.
- Communicate assessments effectively to allow action.

Diagrammatic representations of these activities are also specified [30].

6.5.4   The Vancouver Institute for Visual Analytics

The Vancouver Institute for Visual Analytics (VIVA) [31] is a joint research institute between Simon Fraser University, the University of British Columbia, and the British Columbia Institute of Technology. In 2007, the Boeing Company provided an industrial research grant to Simon Fraser University and the University of British Columbia to study visual analytics. Its objectives were to disseminate visual analytics research results to government and business organizations and to detail how visual analytics might be used within Boeing. A further grant was provided in 2010 to establish VIVA. Training courses, seminars, and a Summer School are provided in visual analytics by VIVA to students, researchers, SMEs, and industrial employees to enable these tools to be used to solve current problems.

6.5.5   The Visual Analytics Research and Development Consortium of Canada

The Visual Analytics Research and Development Consortium of Canada (VARDEC) [32] was found in 2013 in cooperation with Mitacs Inc., the Canadian Network for Visual Analytics (CANVAC), and The Boeing Company. Other founding Canadian member companies include nGrain (Canada) Corporation and Convergent Manufacturing Technologies. The objective of the Visual Analytics Research and Development Consortium of Canada (VARDEC) is to develop and commercialize visual analytics products. It links together major aerospace companies and Small and Medium Enterprises (SMEs) to migrate academic research and development into products and services. Industry-led projects in the academy and research laboratories provide the basis ongoing development.

VARDEC complies with the Government of Canada's Industrial and Technological Benefits (ITB) agreements with international partners, such as The Boeing Company, by supporting investments in modern technology which can benefit the Canadian economy.

6.5.6   Brazilian Visual Analytics Initiative

The Brazilian Visual Analytics Initiative (BRAVA) [33] aims at leveraging the collaborative research in the field of *VA* and promoting the networking between Brazilian and Canadian researchers.

6.5.7   European Union

VisMaster [34] was a European Coordination Action Project focused on the research discipline of visual analytics. Its objective was to address the challenge of increasing amounts of data and be able to utilize it effectively for technological progress and business success. It culminated in the publication "Mastering the Information Age: Solving Problems with Visual Analytics" (Keim et al. [35]).

6.5.8   UK

The University of Oxford e-Research Centre uses Visual Analytics for big data [36]. It regards visual analytics as based on the following assertions:

- *Statistical methods alone cannot convey an adequate amount of information for humans to make informed decisions—hence the need for visualization.*
- *Algorithms alone cannot encode an adequate amount of human knowledge about relevant concepts, facts, and contexts—hence the need for interaction.*
- *Visualization alone cannot effectively manage levels of details about the data or prioritize different information in the data—hence the need for analysis and interaction.*
- *Direct interaction with data alone isn't scalable to the amount of data available—hence the need for analysis and visualization* [36].

6.6   Sample Applications

Visual analytics is relevant to a variety of application domains, and particularly to those involving large datasets, real-time data, heterogeneous data, and areas where the data are complex, ambiguous, or conflicting. These areas include the physical, biological sciences and medical sciences, security, climate and geological monitoring, and commerce. A brief outline of a number of applications is given here [37] while recognizing that static pictures cannot do justice to the nature of applications which are often interactive and in real time. Therefore, these descriptions and illustrations are only indicative.

Sun et al. [38] identified five categories of application as follows:

- Space and time,
- Multivariate,
- Text,
- Graph and network, and
- Others.

These application categories were then related to the most appropriate steps in the visual analytics process: user interaction, analysis, and visual mapping.

6.6.1   Weather and Climate Monitoring

Monitoring weather and climate involves collecting large amounts of real-time data from remote sensors positioned at various points around the globe and in satellites. This data can be input into various climate models. This visual approach assisted the analysts to interpret the data and gain insight into factors governing the climate and climate change.

6.6.2   Visual Analysis of Social Media Data

Schreck and Keim [39] detail how visual analysis may be used in the area of social media.

6.7   Current Research and Development

Areas of current research and development may be exemplified to some extent by the publications at the annual IEEE visualization conference. In the 2018 conference [40], the papers were grouped into the following themes for the three components of the conference: Visual Analytics Science and Technology (VAST), Scientific Visualization (SciVis), and Information Visualization (InfoVis). These themes are detailed in Table 6.2.

Table 6.2 indicates the variety of research and development that is being done nationally and internationally. A number of the above themes could appear in more than one column, but researchers who produced papers for review would normally come from one of the three constituent areas and would submit them to their preferred conference. However, when the themes are examined as a whole, it is clear that this is somewhat arbitrary. For example, many of the themes in SciVis and InfoVis would be relevant to the research in VAST. The areas of interaction and applications (the italic text in Table 6.2) are common to all three areas. Although perception and cognition are key aspects in the field of information visualization (i.e., how is a particular visual representation to be interpreted by a user?), they are just as relevant for visual analytics and scientific visualization, where visual images have to be interpreted at some stage in the analysis. The principal differences in the three areas would appear to be as follows. In visual analytics, a primary objective is to discover relationships and anomalies in datasets particularly when they are very large or in real time. In scientific visualization, the objective is to discover aspects in data representing physical processes or physical objects which result in greater understanding of the laws governing such processes. For information visualization, the objective is to understand how information is assimilated by humans so that it can be portrayed accurately and appropriately in various kinds of visual images from different application domains.

The top ten interaction challenges in extreme-scale visual analytics are outlined by Wong et al. [41, 42].

Table 6.2 Principal themes in the research papers at IEEE Visualization 2018 (with overlapping areas indicated in italic text)

Visual Analytics Science and Technology (VAST)	Scientific Visualization (SciVis)	Information Visualization (InfoVis)
Evaluation and theory	Flow features	Multiple dimensions
Spatiotemporal data	Biological *applications*	Evaluation and *applications*
ensemble and provenance	Biomedical visualization	Time
text	Volume visualization	Graphs and trees
Applications	Space and physics	Devices: Small and large
High-dimensional data	tensors	Text and communication
Security, privacy, and	Scalable techniques	Immersive analytics
anomaly	Topology, geometry, and	Design and Storytelling
Interactive analytics and	precision	*Interaction*
design	*Interaction* and multivariate	Perception and Cognition 1
Deep learning	data	Perception and Cognition 2
Graph and image	Time-varying data	Uncertainty and error
explainable machine learning		
event, sequence, and machine		
learning		

6.8 Has Visual Analytics Subsumed Information Visualization and Scientific Visualization?

As noted earlier, interaction and applications are functions which are common across all the areas of visualization. Thus, there are overlapping functions and goals with the three visualizations. Currently, there is no general agreement on the boundaries between the three areas. However, each area may be characterized as follows [9]:

- *Scientific visualization deals with data that has a natural geometric structure (e.g., MRI data, wind flows).*
- *Information visualization handles abstract data structures such as trees or graphs.*
- *Visual analytics is especially concerned with coupling interactive visual representations with underlying analytical processes (e.g., statistical procedures, data mining techniques) such that high-level, complex activities can be effectively performed (e.g., sense making, reasoning, decision making).*

Visual analytics seeks to marry techniques from information visualization with techniques from computational transformation and analysis of data. Information visualization forms part of the direct interface between user and machine, amplifying human cognitive capabilities. These capabilities of information visualization, combined with computational data analysis, can be applied to analytic reasoning to support the sense-making process [9].

Therefore, there is a degree of interdependence between visual analytics and the other two areas: scientific visualization for data where modeling is required, and information visualization for effective image representation and interaction paradigms to facilitate user sensemaking. From this perspective, therefore, visual analytics subsumes key aspects of the other two areas. Software companies appear to be using the single-term data visualization to cover many areas without necessarily specifying any primary functions. Thus, user assessment and selection of software need to take into account the functions required and also perform user-centered evaluations as detailed earlier.

6.9 The Future

Heer [43] noted the following deficiencies with regard to current data visualizations and what needs to be done to improve them:

- Many images lack perceptual principles.
- Need to augment analysis in the most productive ways and accomplish better decision-making.
- Rankings of visual perception of visual encodings (for comparing quantities from least accurate to most accurate) indicate that position is the most effective representation (e.g., therefore, it can be useful to show bar charts alongside an area map).

- Rethink user interfaces for data visualization. Not specifying a variety of charts for the user to manually select from. It is better to automatically provide a chart based on the data; the user can then drill down for more detail.
- Need new end user exploration tools.
- Move from specification to exploration.
- Show data variation not design variation. Many current images just show alternative designs for the visualization of the same data.
- Users need tools to exercise skepticism and consider new questions.

Therefore, the way forward needs to be characterized by accomplishing transitions as follows:

- From designers to decision-makers.
- From specification to exploration.
- From design variation to data variation.

6.10   Conclusions

This chapter has reviewed the development and advancement of visual analytics and its relationship to scientific visualization and information visualization. Its importance as a tool for the exploration and sensemaking of large datasets has been outlined. When comparing the wide variety of visual analytics products currently available, it is important to consider the functions available, their intended application domains, and how the software is going to be used. Thus, it is advisable to perform a user-centered evaluation as detailed by Scholtz [22]. Current research development in visual analytics has been reviewed and possible future directions outlined.

Further Reading

Kang, Y. and Stasko, J. Examining the Use of a Visual Analytics System for Sense-making Tasks: Case Studies with Domain Experts, IEEE Transactions on Visualization and Computer Graphics, Vol 18, No 12, pp 2869–2878 IEEE, Los Alamitos, CA (2012). Online at—http://web.cse.ohio-state.edu/~machiraju.1/teaching/CSE5544/Visweek2012/vast/papers/kang.pdf
Ward, M. Grinstein, G. and Keim, D. Interactive Data Visualization: Foundations, Techniques, and Applications, 2nd edition, A.K. Peters/CRC Press, Boca Raton, FL (2015).
In addition, a number of the vendors who support visual analytics applications offer tutorials on visual analytics which are set in their context of their own software.

References

1. Newton, I.: Philosophiæ Naturalis Principia Mathematica (1687). (Translation into English: Newton, I. Newton's Principia, Forgotten Books, 2nd ed, 2018, pp 584)
2. ENIAC—Electronic Numerical Integrator and Computer. https://en.wikipedia.org/wiki/ENIAC
3. EDSAC—Electronic delay storage automatic calculator. https://en.wikipedia.org/wiki/Electronic_delay_storage_automatic_calculator, https://www.computerhope.com/issues/ch000984.htm
4. Bowden, B.V. (ed.): Faster than Thought: A Symposium on Digital Computing Machines. Pitman, London, UK (1953)
5. Kuhn, T.: The Structure of Scientific Revolutions: 50th Anniversary Edition. University of Chicago Press, Chicago, IL (2012), Originally published 1962
6. McCormick, B.H., de Fanti, T.A., Brown, M.D.: Visualization in scientific computing. Comput. Graph. **21**(6) (1987) (ACM Siggraph, ACM, New York). https://www.evl.uic.edu/core.php?mod=4&type=3&indi=348
7. Hennessy J.L., Patterson, D.A., Lin, H.S. (eds.): Information Technology for Counterterrorism: Immediate Actions and Future Possibilities. National Academy of Sciences, Washington, D.C. (2003). https://www.nap.edu/catalog/10640/information-technology-for-counterterrorism-immediate-actions-and-future-possibilities
8. NVAC—http://www.vacommunity.org/item1, https://vis.pnnl.gov/
9. Thomas, J.J., Cook, K.A. (eds.): Illuminating the Path: The Research and Development Agenda for Visual Analytics. IEEE Computer Society Press, Los Alamitos, CA (2005). Online PDF of the book https://www.hsdl.org/?abstract&did=485291, https://ils.unc.edu/courses/2017_fall/inls641_001/books/RD_Agenda_VisualAnalytics.pdf, https://vis.pnnl.gov
10. Henke, N., Bughin, J., Chui, M., Manyika, J., Saleh, T., Wiseman, B., Sethupathy, G.: The Age of Analytics: Competing in a Data Driven World. McKinsey Global Institute (2016). https://www.mckinsey.com/~/media/McKinsey/Business%20Functions/McKinsey%20Analytics/Our%20Insights/The%20age%20of%20analytics%20Competing%20in%20a%20data%20driven%20world/MGI-The-Age-of-Analytics-Full-report.ashx
11. Fisher, D., Deline, R., Czerwinski, M., Drucker, S.: Interactions with Big Data analytics. ACM Interact. **19**(3), 50–59 (2012) (ACM, New York, NY). https://dl.acm.org/citation.cfm?id=2168943
12. Hong, S.H., Ma, K.L., Koyamada, K.: Big Data Visual Analytics—NII Shonan Meeting Report (2015). https://pdfs.semanticscholar.org/45ec/4934ee034a5839f4e657089ac865f0baa8ff.pdf
13. https://en.wikipedia.org/wiki/Visual_analytics
14. Keim, D., Mansmann, F., Schneidewind, J., Thomas, J., Ziegler, H.: In: Simoff, S.J. Bohlen, M.H. Mazeika, A. (eds.) Visual Data Mining: Theory, Techniques and Tools for Visual Analytics, pp. 76–90. LNCS 4404, Springer, Cham, Switzerland (2008). https://kops.uni-konstanz.de/bitstream/handle/123456789/5631/Visual_Analytics_Scope_and_Challenges.pdf?sequence=1
15. Scholtz, J., Burtner, R., Cook, K.A.: Visual analytics 101. In: Proceedings of the 2016 CHI Conference on Human Factors in Computing Systems (CHI EA'16), pp. 955–958. ACM Press, New York, NY (2016). https://doi.org/10.1145/2851581.2856674
16. Keim, D., Andrienko, G., Fekete, J.D., Görg, C., Kohlhammer, J., Melançon, G.: Visual analytics: definition, process, and challenges. In: Kerren, A., Stasko, J.T., Fekete, J.D., North, C. (eds.) Information Visualization: Human-Centered Issues and Perspectives, pp. 154–175. LNCS 4950. Springer, Cham, Switzerland (2008). https://hal-lirmm.ccsd.cnrs.fr/lirmm-00272779/document, https://link.springer.com/chapter/10.1007/978-3-540-70956-5_7
17. Yang, Q., Wu, X.: 10 challenging problems in data mining research. Int. J. Inf. Technol. Decis. Mak. **05**(04), 597–604 (2006) (World Scientific). https://doi.org/10.1142/S0219622006002258, https://www.worldscientific.com/worldscinet/ijitdm
18. Järvinen, P., Puolamäki, K., Siltanen, P., Ylikerälä. M.: Visual Analytics—Final Report (2009). https://www.vtt.fi/inf/pdf/workingpapers/2009/W117.pdf

19. Zhang, L., Stoffel, A., Behrisch, M., Mittelstaedt, S., Schreck, T., Pomp, R., Weber, S., Last, H., Keim, D.: Visual analytics for the Big Data era—a comparative review of state-of-the-art commercial systems. In: IEEE Conference on Visual Analytics Science and Technology (2012). http://web.cse.ohio-state.edu/~machiraju.1/teaching/CSE5544/Visweek2012/vast/papers/zhang.pdf

20. Behrisch, M., Streeb, D., Stoffel, F., Seebacher, D., Matejek, B., Weber, S.H., Mittelstaedt, S., Pfister, H., Keim, D.: Commercial visual analytics systems-advances in the Big Data analytics field. In: IEEE Transactions on Visualization and Computer Graphics. IEEE, Hoboken, NJ (2018). https://ieeexplore.ieee.org/document/8423105/

21. Visual Analytics Market worth 6.51 Billion USD by 2022. https://www.marketsandmarkets.com/PressReleases/visual-analytics.asp,   https://www.marketsandmarkets.com/Market-Reports/visual-analytics-market-147932448.html,   https://www.prnewswire.com/news-releases/the-global-visual-analytics-market-size-is-expected-to-reach-77-billion-by-2023-300578153.html

22. Scholtz J.: User-centered evaluation of visual analytics. In: Synthesis Lectures on Visualization Series. Morgan & Claypool, San Rafael, CA (2017). https://doi.org/10.2200/s00797ed1v01y201709vis009

23. Harger, J.R., Crossno, P.J.: Comparison of open source visual analytics toolkits. In: Proceedings of SPIE—The International Society for Optical Engineering, vol. 8294 (2012). https://www.sandia.gov/~pjcross/papers/Part1.pdf

24. Managing large research activities (UK). https://epsrc.ukri.org/funding/managing/largeactivities/

25. NSF funded Graphics and Visualization Centre: https://cs.brown.edu/stc/STC_Overview.html, https://cs.brown.edu/stc/home.html, https://ohiostate.pressbooks.pub/graphicshistory/chapter/5-5-other-labs-and-nsf-technology-center/ (1991)

26. Center for Visualization and Data Analytics, Homeland Security University Programs. https://www.hsuniversityprograms.org/centers/emeritus/cvada-data-visual-analytics/, https://www.dhs.gov/sites/default/files/publications/Center%20for%20Visualization%20and%20Data%20Analytics-CVADA.pdf, https://www.dhs.gov/science-and-technology/hsarpa/da-e

27. USA Visualization and Analytics Centers. Overview: https://wiki.cs.umd.edu/semvast/images/2/2e/TSG_Flier.pdf; Stanford University: https://news.stanford.edu/pr/2005/pr-hanrahan-020905.html; VACET: http://www.vacet.org/contact.html; https://icl.utk.edu/ctwatch/quarterly/print.php%3Fp=93.html; Purdue University: https://engineering.purdue.edu/Engr/Research/LabsFacilities/RVAC; Georgia Tech and UNC-Charlotte: http://srvac.cc.gatech.edu/; https://srvac.uncc.edu/; Pennsylvania State University: https://www.geovista.psu.edu/NEVAC/

28. VACCINE: https://www.purdue.edu/discoverypark/vaccine/

29. http://www.canvac.org/CANVAC_public/index.php/about/overview,   http://www.vacommunity.org/item10, http://www.canvac.org/CANVAC_public/index.php/about/partner-organizations

30. http://www.canvac.org/CANVAC_public/index.php/about/visual-analytics

31. http://viva.sfu.ca/index.php/about/viva, http://viva.sfu.ca/index.php/training

32. http://vardec.ca/about-vardec

33. http://seer.ufrgs.br/index.php/jis/article/download/41856/26632,   http://boeing.mediaroom.com/2012-04-03-Boeing-Mitacs-Sponsor-Advanced-Technology-Research-with-Brazil-and-Canada

34. http://www.vismaster.eu/, http://www.visual-analytics.eu/

35. Keim, D., Kohlhammer, J., Ellis, G., Mansmann, F.: Mastering the Information Age: Solving Problems with Visual Analytics (2010). http://www.vismaster.eu/wp-content/uploads/2010/11/VisMaster-book-lowres.pdf

36. Oxford e-Research Centre: http://www.oerc.ox.ac.uk/projects/visual-analytics-big-data, http://idc.cs.mdx.ac.uk/, http://valcri.org/

37. http://viva.sfu.ca/index.php/about/visual-analytics

38. Sun, G.D., Wu, Y.C., Liang, R.H., Liu, S.X.: A survey of visual analytics techniques and applications: state-of-the-art research and future challenges. J. Comput. Sci. Technol. **28**(5), 852–867 (2013). https://doi.org/10.1007/s11390-013-1383-8. http://www.cad.zju.edu.cn/home/ycwu/Files/va_survey.pdf

39. Schreck, T., Keim, D.: Visual analysis of social media data. IEEE Comput. **46**(5), 68–75 (2013) (IEEE Computer Society). http://doi.ieeecomputersociety.org/10.1109/MC.2012.430. https://www.computer.org/csdl/mags/co/2013/05/mco2013050068.html

40. Session and Paper Titles for the VAST2018 Conference. http://ieeevis.org/year/2018/info/overview-amp-topics/papers-sessions

41. Wong, P.C., Shen, H.-W., Chen, C.: Top ten interaction challenges in extreme-scale visual analytics. In: Dill, J., et al. (eds.) Expanding the Frontiers of Visual Analytics and Visualization, pp. 197–207. Springer, Cham, Switzerland (2012). https://www.springer.com/gb/book/9781447128038

42. Wong, P.C., Shen, H.-W., Johnson, C.R., Chen, C., Ross, R.B.: The top 10 interaction challenges in extreme-scale visual analytics. IEEE Comput. Graph. Appl. **32**(4), 63–67 (2012) (IEEE). https://www.ncbi.nlm.nih.gov/pmc/articles/PMC3907777/

43. Heer, J.: The future of data visualization (Strata and Hadoop, 2015) video 10mins Co-Founder of Trifacta: "Charting a Path Forward: The Future of Data Visualization". https://www.youtube.com/watch?v=vc1bq0qIKoA

Chapter 7
Data Science Institutes and Data Centers

Rae Earnshaw

Abstract Optimum ways of addressing large data volumes across a variety of disciplines have led to the formation of national and institutional Data Science Institutes and Centers. The objectives and functions of such institutes and centers are summarized. In reflecting the driver of national priority, they are able to attract academic support within their institutions to bring together interdisciplinary expertise to address a wide variety of datasets from disciplines such as astronomy, bioinformatics, engineering, science, medicine, social science, and the humanities. All are generating increasing volumes of data, often in real time, and require efficient and effective solutions. The opportunities and challenges of data science are presented. The processes of knowledge discovery in data science often require new methods and software, new organizational arrangements, and new skills in order to be effective. Data science centers and institutes provide a focus for the development and implementation of such new structures and arrangements for the development of appropriate facilities, with academic leadership and professional support. These are summarized and reviewed.

Keywords Infrastructure for data science · Interdisciplinary research collaboration · Artificial intelligence · Machine learning · Data mining · Statistical inference · Data management · Data visualization · Cultural change · Reward models

7.1 Introduction

Increasing volumes of data in a wide variety of disciplines are forcing academic, industry, and government to address optimum ways to analyze such data effectively. To assist with this, institutions are seeking to provide collaborative research environments in order to increase critical mass and be more competitive for research funding and graduate students. Supercomputers have been used for a number of years to process data from the physical sciences relatively successfully, but the data

R. Earnshaw et al., *Data Science and Visual Computing*,
SpringerBriefs in Advanced Information and Knowledge Processing,
https://doi.org/10.1007/978-3-030-24367-8_7

science revolution caused by the rapid increase in data from a variety of sources could not be satisfactorily addressed solely within the existing disciplines and structures. Therefore, it has been necessary to initiate a transformation of both the processes of knowledge discovery, and also the institutional environments in which this discovery takes place.

7.2   Sources of Data

The Moore-Sloan Data Science Environments comprising New York University, University of California at Berkeley, and the University of Washington (2018) outlined the key elements of a data science environment and also included a summary of current data source as follows:

> *Consider the scale and complexity of data sources coming online: simulations of scale and resolution unimaginable only a few years ago (e.g., global climate models, universe-scale n-body simulations), networks of tiny but powerful sensors (e.g., on the seafloor; in the forest canopy; in living organisms; in buildings, roads and bridges), high-bandwidth remote-sensing platforms (e.g., satellites like Terra and Aqua with Moderate Resolution Imaging Spectroradiometers, telescopes used for survey astronomy projects like the Sloan Digital Sky Survey and the Large Synoptic Survey Telescope), high-throughput laboratory instruments (e.g., gene sequencers, micro-and macro-scopic imaging equipment, flow cytometers, mass spectrometers), city-wide urban sensing platforms (e.g., connected vehicles, environmental sensors, ubiquitous cameras), repositories of open government data driven by a new culture of transparency, and social science data created in digital form (e.g., global economic indicators; social network data; consumer activities, including purchasing, mobile phone usage, and internet clickstreams). These advances share a common trait: they produce data with relentlessly increasing volume, velocity, and variety—data that must be captured, transported, stored, organized, curated, accessed, mined, visualized, and interpreted. Data-intensive discovery, or data science, is a cornerstone of 21st-century discovery [1].*

7.3   Rationale for Data Science Institutes and Centers

The drivers for the creation of centers to provide a focus for these initiatives include many of the following:

- Alignment with national and international priorities.
- Provision of a top-slice of the institution's budget to support the center.
- Ability to attract significant grant support from funding agencies with priorities in the area of big data.
- Ability to attract advanced level skills and expertise.
- Infrastructure to provide a secure environment to deal with large datasets.
- Opportunities to support research collaboration on big data across an institution.
- Provide research expertise in machine learning, data mining, data visualization, data management, and statistics.

- Provision of interdisciplinary expertise to address a wide variety of application areas.
- Provide an appropriate environment to give support for major national initiatives.
- Gain local and national industry support.
- Gain civic interest and support.
- Opportunities for graduate students to work on a variety of research problems.
- Attractive environment to deliver Masters courses in Data Analytics.

Many institutions with significant investments in research and development have already set up such centers and others have plans to do so. Because the senior management of the university has decided such an institute/center is a high priority for the institution, it often provides funding for the setting up and operation of the facility. It is therefore not a direct charge on existing faculty budgets. Many such centers do not take faculty from existing faculty structures but are an additional resource center which is more centralized within the institution and where faculty and researchers may come together to access and share computational resources, expertise, and ideas.

7.4   Objectives and Functions of Data Science Institutes and Centers

Tables 7.1, 7.2, 7.3, and 7.4 show a sample of institutes and centers in a variety of institutions and countries. These are not listed in any order of priority or importance. The tables are only indicative and are not intended to be representative of particular countries, nor are all countries included.

A common driver in all the above organizations is the continually increasing sizes of the data to process in many disciplines.

There is a high degree of commonality in the objectives and functions of the data institutes and centers as illustrated in Tables 7.1, 7.2, 7.3, and 7.4. These include the following:

- To advance R&D in data analytics in all disciplines.
- Enable all fields, professions, and sectors to develop through the application of data science.
- Connect government, industry, and academia.
- Accelerate research, innovation, and training in data-intensive science.
- Support interdisciplinary research.
- Address current problems in society and the environment.
- Develop new mathematical and statistical theory, and quantitative and computational methods.
- Support graduate studies in data science (e.g., Masters degrees in Data Analytics and research).
- Support postdoctoral researchers.

Table 7.1 A sample of Institutes and Centers in Data Science in the USA

USA	Institute/Center	Objectives and functions
University of California at Berkeley	Institute for Data Science https://bids.berkeley.edu/	Facilitate and nurture data-intensive science Advancing scientific discovery through collaboration across research domains
University of California at San Diego	Halıcıoğlu Data Science Institute https://datascience.ucsd.edu/ https://datascience.ucsd.edu/about/index.html https://youtu.be/dHu1CSADOZQ (video 5 min)	By developing new tools and educating the next generation of data scientists, our goal is to improve our quality of life as digital data continues its integration into the infrastructure of commerce, health care, government, and education
Columbia	Data Science Institute https://datascience.columbia.edu/	To advance the state of the art in data science To transform all fields, professions, and sectors through the application of data science To ensure the responsible use of data to benefit society
Georgia Tech	Institute for Data Engineering and Science http://ideas.gatech.edu/	Data science foundations, and data-driven discovery Connect government, industry, and academia to advance foundational research, and accelerate the adoption of big data technology
MIT	Institute for Data, Systems, and Society https://idss.mit.edu/	Addressing complex societal challenges by advancing education and research at the intersection of statistics, data science, information and decision systems, and social sciences
New York University	Center for Data Science https://cds.nyu.edu/	Tools to harness the power of big data

(continued)

Table 7.1 (continued)

USA	Institute/Center	Objectives and functions
Purdue University	Integrative Data Science Institute https://www.purdue.edu/data-science/	The initiative focuses on advancing the frontiers of research and the application of data science to pressing, socially relevant issues, as well as a new campus-wide, transformational data science education initiative
Vanderbilt	Data Science Institute https://news.vanderbilt.edu/2018/08/13/vanderbilt-data-science-institute-launched/	Promotes and facilitates data-driven research Advance foundational research and data science skills across campus and to leverage the university's collaborative culture
Washington	eScience Institute https://escience.washington.edu/ http://data.washington.edu/	Advancing data-intensive discovery in all fields Answer fundamental questions through the use of large, complex, and noisy data

Table 7.2 A sample of Institutes and Centers in Data Science in Canada

Canada	Institute/Center	Objectives and functions
University of British Columbia	Data Science Institute https://dsi.ubc.ca/about	Catalyze data science innovation Incubate and accelerate research, innovation, and training in data-intensive science
Carleton	Institute for Data Science https://carleton.ca/cuids/	Interdisciplinary research and graduate studies in data science
Montreal	Data Science Institute https://datascienceinstitute.org/	Data science solutions and methodologies to find innovative solutions to the complex problems of our customers
Simon Fraser University	Key Big Data initiative https://www.sfu.ca/key/ Research Data Center (RDC) http://www.sfu.ca/rdc.html	Tools, training, and expertise to unlock the potential of big data RDC is part of the British Columbia Inter-university Research Data Centre, supported by partner universities, SSHRC/CIHR, and Statistics Canada to facilitate access to data for crucial social research

Table 7.3 A sample of Institutes and Centers in Data Science in the UK

UK	Institute/Center	Objectives and functions
Alan Turing Institute	https://www.turing.ac.uk/	National Institute for Data Science and Artificial Intelligence is to make great leaps in research in order to change the world for the better
Ada Lovelace Institute	https://www.turing.ac.uk/news/turing-partners-nuffield-foundation-announce-new-ps5-million-ada-lovelace-institute	Ensure data and Artificial Intelligence (AI) work for people and society
Cambridge	Big Data Strategic Research Initiative https://www.bigdata.cam.ac.uk/	Applications ranging from astronomy and bioinformatics to medicine, social science, and the humanities Research also addresses important issues around law, ethics, and economics in order to apply big data to solve challenging problems for society
Edinburgh	Edinburgh Data Science https://www.ed.ac.uk/data-science	Bring the university community together with an emphasis on communication, sharing of best practice, and future development
Exeter	Institute for Data Science and Artificial Intelligence https://www.exeter.ac.uk/idsai/	Innovate new means of interrogating and understanding data and then to innovate and apply cutting-edge data analytical methodologies to diverse questions
Imperial	Data Science Institute https://www.imperial.ac.uk/data-science/	Collecting, preparing, managing, analyzing, interpreting, and visualizing large and complex datasets
Lancaster	Data Science Institute http://www.lancaster.ac.uk/dsi/	Interdisciplinary approach to contemporary data-driven research challenges
Leeds	Leeds Institute for Data Analytics https://lida.leeds.ac.uk/	Brings together applied research groups and data scientists from all disciplines, opening up new opportunities to understand health and human behavior and casting light on the action required to tackle a wide range of social and environmental problems

(continued)

Table 7.3 (continued)

UK	Institute/Center	Objectives and functions
Manchester	Data Science Institute http://www.datascience.manchester.ac.uk/	Basic research in advanced data analytics and address data-driven research in Health and Biology, Social and Policy, Environment, Urban, Business and Management and the Physical Sciences
Oxford	Big Data Institute https://www.bdi.ox.ac.uk/	Analysis of large, complex, heterogeneous datasets for research into the causes and consequences, prevention, and treatment of disease
Oxford	Oxford Internet Institute https://www.oii.ox.ac.uk/study/courses/big-data-analytics/	Collect, clean, analyze, model, and interpret social science data
University College, London	Big Data Institute https://www.ucl.ac.uk/big-data/bdi	Investigation of new technologies and analytics as applied to scholarly content and data
University College, London	Centre for Data Science http://www.ucl.ac.uk/big-data/	Develop new mathematical and statistical theory, and quantitative and computational methods, to help make sense of large, complex datasets

Table 7.4 A sample of Institutes and Centers in Data Science in France, Switzerland, Singapore, and Australia

	Institute/Center	Objectives and functions
France		
Paris/Nice	Data Science Tech Institute https://www.datasciencetech. institute/	Graduate School in France for Applied Data Science, Big Data and Data Engineering
Switzerland		
	Swiss Data Science Center https://datascience.ch/	Accompany the academic community and the industrial sector in their data science journey, putting to work AI and ML and facilitating the multidisciplinary exchange of data and knowledge
Singapore		
National University of Singapore	Institute of Data Science http://ids.nus.edu.sg/ http://datascience.sg/ http://sdsc.sg/	Leverage and strengthen data science expertise for transdisciplinary and translational research into important real-life problems and education of the next generation of data scientists
Australia		
Monash University	Centre for Data Science https://www.monash.edu/it/ our-research/research-centres-and-labs/centre-for-data-science	Work with industry, government, and community partners to develop effective data-driven solutions with impact and research expertise. Areas of research expertise include data governance, data management and data archiving, data analytics and visualization in the digital humanities, community, cultural heritage, and not-for-profit sectors
Swinburne	Data Science Research Institute https://www.swinburne.edu. au/research-institutes/data-science/	Lead the emerging academic inter-discipline that marries the physical sciences with statistics and computer science. The core business is developing cutting-edge methodologies for handling and analyzing large and complex datasets

7.5 Graduate Education and Research

Most of the institutes and centers in the tables also provide a focus for graduate students to study for a Masters degree in Data Analytics and/or to do graduate research for a Ph.D. Many have access to faculty expertise for research and teaching by affiliated appointments with their home department/faculty, or by other linking arrangements such as becoming an Academic Fellow in the institute [2]. Many employ data scientists at Ph.D. level for the research programs within the institute, although attention has to be paid to the issue of the status of such staff within an academic institution to ensure that their career paths and prospects are supported.

7.6 National Centers in Data Science

Many countries have identified big data as an area requiring significant development and support. Their governments established working groups to evaluate the current trends in applications data and the needs and requirements of organizations and businesses, in order to evaluate what resources and skills are needed to meet current and future requirements. Some countries have established National Centers to lead and coordinate R&D in the field (for example, [3–5]).

7.6.1 USA

In the USA, the National Consortium for Data Science (NCDS) was established in 2013 as a collaboration of leaders in academia, industry, and government to address the data challenges and opportunities of the twenty-first century. The NCDS helps members take advantage of data in ways that result in new jobs and transformative discoveries. Its objective is to enable research, innovation, economic development, and *build a data science community for the economy of the future* [6].

The National Science Foundation (NSF) made a number of strategic recommendations with regard to realizing the potential of data science [7]. This included the following:

- Create Data Science Research Centers.
- Invest in research into Data Science Infrastructure that furthers effective data sharing, data use, and life cycle management.
- Support research into effective reproducibility.

- Fund research into models that underlie evidence-based data policy and decision-making.
- Expand funding into deep learning, smart environments, and other artificial intelligence-empowered areas and their use in data-driven applications.

It also made number of recommendations with regard to education and training, creating collections of datasets, addressing aspects of the Internet of Things (IoT) in areas such as security and data privacy, and addressing architectural issues to support emerging data-intensive tasks.

In February 2018, the NSF announced $30 million in funding through its critical techniques, technologies, and methodologies for Advancing Foundations and Applications of Big Data Sciences and Engineering (BIGDATA) program. The grants were linked with support from Amazon Web Services (AWS), Google Cloud Platform (GCP), and Microsoft Azure, which have each committed up to $3 million in cloud resources for relevant BIGDATA projects over a 3-year period. A key objective of this collaboration is to encourage research projects to focus on large-scale experimentation and scalability studies [8].

Data.gov [9] is a U.S. government website launched in late May 2009 by the then Federal Chief Information Officer (CIO) of the United States, Vivek Kundra. Data.gov aims to improve public access to high value, machine-readable datasets generated by the Executive Branch of the Federal Government. The site is a repository for federal, state, local, and tribal government information, made available to the public.

7.6.2   UK

In the UK, the Alan Turing Institute was established in 2015 to be the national institute for data science and artificial intelligence. It was created by five founding universities—Cambridge, Edinburgh, Oxford, UCL, and Warwick—and the UK Engineering and Physical Sciences Research Council. Eight further universities—Leeds, Manchester, Newcastle, Queen Mary University of London, Birmingham, Exeter, Bristol, and Southampton—joined the institute in 2018. This linking into a UK Research Council and support by leading universities in the UK effectively established it as an important national initiative and resource.

In the UK, the Diamond Report in 2015 [10] made a number of recommendations for improved education in skills with regard to data analytics, and also proposed the following:

> Many breakthroughs in the development of analytical methods and tools have happened at the intersection between different disciplines. An implication is that we need to support interdisciplinary, innovative research projects involving advanced data analytics, statistics and quantitative skills, and that calls for cross–research council collaboration and funding. Our recommendation is for a top slice of the RCUK budget to establish a strategic fund through which interdisciplinary research is funded. RCUK could itself take a strategic and convening role in this space

and

> *There are currently many agencies in the UK exercising leadership to address the skills shortages arising in industry from the data revolution. However, no single body has all the answers to what are system-wide challenges. Collaboration is needed to address the national challenges identified in our research. We call on relevant stakeholders, including the Tech Partnership, the Royal Statistical Society, the UK Commission for Employment and Skills, the E–Infrastructure Leadership Council, the Digital Economy Council, techUK, the ODI, HEFCE and the research and sector skills councils to set up a cross–cutting taskforce around data analytics to identify good practices for education and skills provision and spur collaboration across industry.*

and

> *…grassroots activities could be usefully complemented by a higher visibility network following the example of an organisation like the US National Consortium for Data Science, or Scotland's Data Lab, a £11.3 million initiative supported by the Scottish Funding Council, Highlands and Islands Enterprise and Scottish Enterprise, which 'enables new collaborations between industry, public sector and universities driven by common interests in the exploitation of data science, provides resources and funding to kick start projects, deliver skills and training, and helps to develop the local ecosystem by building a cohesive data science community.' We believe that a data science network along these lines should be developed with involvement from existing communities of analytical practice, the Alan Turing Institute, the Data Lab, the Catapults, and major Data Science institutes at universities like Imperial College, UCL, Manchester and Warwick.*

A report from Nesta in 2015 [11] also proposed the following:

> *The 'big data explosion' requires new analytics skills to transform big datasets into good decisions and innovative products.*

Key findings

- *There isn't a one-size fit all to creating value from data. Our research reveals three types of 'Data active' businesses: Datavores who base their decisions on data and analysis, Data Builders working with big datasets, and Data Mixers who combine data from different sources. We also find 30% of 'Dataphobe' businesses who seem to have given the data revolution a pass.*

- *Data-active companies (especially Datavores and Data Builders) perform better than the Dataphobes. Our econometric analysis reveals that they are over 10% more productive than the Dataphobes after controlling for other factors.*

- *Data-active companies are recruiting more analysts, and combining more disciplines to build a data science capability. This isn't proving easy: For example, two thirds of Datavores struggled to fill at least one vacancy. 80% of them identified problems in at least one skills area. Data-active companies are particularly concerned about the lack of domain knowledge in analysts, the lack of people with the right mix of skills and the lack of experienced analysts.*

- *Technology is changing fast in the data space, and employers are keeping the skills of their data analysts fresh through a variety of approaches. 80% do internal training. Significant proportions (between a third and two thirds) are using innovative training methods like data competitions, online courses and meetups. Only a fifth use universities to train their staff.*

In addition, the Ada Lovelace Institute was set up in the UK in 2018 to coordinate R&D in Artificial Intelligence (AI) and ensure that AI is able to work for people and society [12].

7.7   Opportunities for Data Science Research

One of the principal opportunities of a Data Science Institute is to incorporate major research initiatives. An example of this is at the Leeds Institute for Data Analytics. This hosts the following:

- MRC Medical Bioinformatics Centre (£7 million funding) [13] and
- ESRC Consumer Data Research Centre (£11 million funding) [14].

The MRC Medical Bioinformatics Centre aims to create and sustain the infrastructure, facilities, understanding, and culture changes required to enable groundbreaking and productive bioinformatics research at the interface between the clinic, health records, and high volume molecular and phenotypic datasets. It also collaborates with a wide range of business organizations and healthcare providers. In addition, it has been able to leverage an additional £14 million of funding from other sources.

The Consumer Data Research Centre creates, supplies, and maintains data for a wide range of users [15]. It works with private and public data suppliers to ensure efficient, effective, and safe use of data in social science. It is led by the University of Leeds and University College, London, with partners at the Universities of Liverpool and Oxford. One of its functions is to provide a national service using the data that can be accessed via the data store, such as point of sale receipts, travel records, and market research data. It works with private and public data suppliers to ensure efficient, effective, and safe use of data in the social sciences.

Being able to host national data science research initiatives has the following advantages for a Data Science Institute:

- Provides infrastructure for data storage, access, and analysis.
- Provides a center and focus for data science expertise.
- Opportunities for interdisciplinary collaborations.
- Opportunities for cross-fertilization of ideas across disciplines.
- Able to leverage further research grant funding in associated disciplines.
- Opportunities to attract external sponsorship, endowments, and donations.
- Attract interest within the institution in data science.
- Attractor externally for data scientists and graduate students.
- Attract national and international interest in the research.
- Seminar programs with national and international researchers.

A number of these advantages also apply to a Data Science Institute that does not have an associated national facility under its aegis, but they may not be evident to the same extent. In some cases, the setting up of a Data Science Institute has attracted a national facility; in other cases, the institute has focused initially on a pre-existing national facility within the institution, and then broadened the infrastructure to support other disciplines.

7.8 Challenges in Data Science Research

Data science research faces a number of challenges. These include the following:

- Discipline-based faculties and budgets within academic institutions do not generally support wider ways of working, because they are based on historic structures which can be difficult to change.
- Interdisciplinary collaborations can be difficult to initiate and operate.
- Grant awarding mechanisms can be biased toward single disciplines because of the way the funding agencies are compartmentalized along disciplinary lines.
- Promotion criteria for faculty can be difficult to formulate and agree (particularly for tenure).
- Career advancement within academia can be difficult in interdisciplinary areas.

Harvey [16] lists the current big data challenges as follows:

- Dealing with data growth.
- Generating insights in a timely manner.
- Recruiting and retaining big data talent.
- Integrating disparate data sources.
- Validating data.
- Securing big data.
- Organizational resistance.

Because of the complexity of the analysis of large amounts of data, questions can arise with regard to the verifiability of the results that are obtained. In order to provide confidence in the publication of the results, it is increasingly required that it clearly specifies how they have been obtained, and give access to the data in order that the results can be verified. This can be facilitated by the use of open-source tools and by supporting reuse and open science [17].

The Moore-Sloan Data Science Environments: New York University, UC Berkeley, and the University of Washington (2018) [1] detail the aspects of institutional change that are required in order to implement data science successfully. These include the following factors:

- Career paths and alternative metrics.
- Education and training.
- Software tools, environments, and support.
- Reproducibility and open science.
- Working spaces and culture.
- Ethnography and evaluation.

Earnshaw [18] details the issues associated with interdisciplinary research and development. The following aspects were considered to be potential advantages:

- Further the growth at the boundaries of existing disciplines.
- Potential for knowledge transfer to industry and society.
- Freedom and opportunity in new areas of research and development.
- Publication of significant results.
- Lines of reporting can be more flexible.

The following were considered to be areas where significant challenges could arise:

- Lack of high-ranking interdisciplinary journals and conferences.
- Lack of general respect in the peer community for interdisciplinary research publications—they can be perceived to be "less pure" than those in a single discipline.
- Blue sky research is still perceived to be of higher kudos than anything that may be more applied.
- Applications to grant awarding bodies and agencies—where reviewers from the different disciplines may have different views.
- Reconciling different cultures and working practices in different disciplines.
- Relationship to senior faculty and the university.
- Tenure committee considerations, where criteria are well established for single disciplines but are often not so clear for interdisciplinary research. This can discourage junior faculty from working in this area as it can be perceived as high risk from a career point of view.
- Employment of faculty on part-time or zero-hours contracts.

As interdisciplinary research gains traction, momentum, and international acceptance through initiatives such as data science, it is possible that some of the challenges listed above may be addressed more effectively than has been the case to date.

7.9 Conclusions

The growth in the significance and extent of data from many disciplines has been outlined. This presents a major challenge as it is not possible to analyze this effectively using traditional data processing methods. New approaches are needed, and the opportunities and advantages of data science and Data Science Institutes have been reviewed. Such solutions often require interdisciplinary methods, and therefore effective collaborations are necessary and important in these new environments. These represent a significant shift in the way traditional academic research has been performed within disciplines, and therefore major efforts are needed to address these challenges. However, the rewards are great as the majority of future research and development is likely to be in the context of large datasets which traverse disciplines in the way they arise, and in the methods used to extract verifiable information and knowledge from them.

Further Reading

Grus, J. Data Science from Scratch: First Principles with Python, O'Reilly Media, Sebastopol, CA (2015). http://shop.oreilly.com/product/0636920033400.do
Graduate Programs in Computer Science. https://www.datasciencegraduateprograms.com/
External Funding Opportunities. https://ics.psu.edu/resources-for-researchers/external-funding-opportunities/
NSF Critical Techniques, Technologies and Methodologies for Advancing Foundations and Applications of Big Data Sciences and Engineering (BIGDATA), USA. https://www.nsf.gov/funding/pgm_summ.jsp?pims_id=504767
National Institutes for Health (NIH) Computational Genomics and Data Science Program, USA. https://www.genome.gov/10001735/computational-genomics-and-data-science-program/
Examples of Big Data Initiatives and Funding Projects. https://www.icpsr.umich.edu/icpsrweb/content/DSDR/bigdata-examples.html
Big Data, Arts and Humanities Research Council (AHRC), UK. https://ahrc.ukri.org/research/fundedthemesandprogrammes/themes/digitaltransformations/bigdata/
Engineering and Physical Sciences Research Council (EPSRC), UK
New Approaches to Data Science, 2016. https://epsrc.ukri.org/files/funding/calls/2016/newapproachestodatascienceinfodayslides/, https://epsrc.ukri.org/funding/calls/newapproachestodatascience/, https://www.ubdc.ac.uk/news-media/2018/january/big-data-project-gets-3m-funding-boost/
Biotechnology and Biological *Sciences* Research Council (BBSRC), UK
Data Driven Biology. https://bbsrc.ukri.org/funding/grants/priorities/data-driven-biology/

References

1. Creating Institutional Change in Data Science, The Moore-Sloan Data Science Environments: New York University, UC Berkeley, and the University of Washington (2018). https://bids.berkeley.edu/news/how-create-institutional-change-data-science-and-encourage-data-driven-discovery, http://msdse.org/files/Creating_Institutional_Change.pdf
2. Imperial: https://www.imperial.ac.uk/data-science/get-involved/dsi-academic-fellowship/ (2018)
3. UK Government Transformation Strategy, 2017–20. https://www.gov.uk/government/publications/government-transformation-strategy-2017-to-2020/government-transformation-strategy
4. UK Government Digital Service: https://www.gov.uk/government/organisations/government-digital-service
5. Turing Institute: https://www.turing.ac.uk/about-us (2015)
6. Benefits of the public-private partnership for NCDS. https://datascienceconsortium.org/, https://www.hpcuserforum.com/presentations/virginia-april2015/KnowlesNCDS-overview.pdf
7. Berman, F., Rutenbar, R., Christenson, H., Davidson, S., Estrin, D., Franklin, M., Hailpern, B., Martonosi, M., Raghavan, P., Stodden, V., Szalay, A.: Realizing the Potential of Data Science, Final Report from the NSF Computer and Information Science and Engineering Advisory Committee Data Science Working Group (2017). https://www.nsf.gov/cise/ac-data-science-report/CISEACDataScienceReport1.19.17.pdf, https://www.nsf.gov/events/event_group.jsp?group_id=20023&org=NSF
8. NSF: https://www.hpcwire.com/2018/02/07/nsf-adds-30m-bigdata-program-aws-google-azure-participate/, https://www.nsf.gov/news/news_summ.jsp?org=NSF&cntn_id=244450&preview=false (2018)
9. https://en.wikipedia.org/wiki/Data.gov
10. Diamond, Sir I.: Making the most of Data: Data skills training in English Universities (2015). https://www.universitiesuk.ac.uk/policy-and-analysis/reports/Documents/2015/making-the-most-of-data-training-skills-english-universities.pdf, https://www.universitiesuk.ac.uk/news/Pages/report-looks-at-whether-universities-produce-graduates-with-data-skills.aspx
11. Nesta: Talent and the Data Revolution (2015). https://www.nesta.org.uk/report/skills-of-the-datavores-talent-and-the-data-revolution/, https://media.nesta.org.uk/documents/skills_of_the_datavores.pdf
12. Ada Lovelace Institute: https://www.turing.ac.uk/news/turing-partners-nuffield-foundation-announce-new-ps5-million-ada-lovelace-institute (2018)
13. MRC Medical Bioinformatics Centre: https://lida.leeds.ac.uk/research/mbc/, https://gtr.ukri.org/projects?ref=MR%2FL01629X%2F1
14. ESRC Consumer Data Research Centre: https://lida.leeds.ac.uk/research/consumer-data-research-centre/
15. Consumer Data Research Centre Data Service: https://data.cdrc.ac.uk/
16. Harvey, C.: Big Data Challenges, Datamation (2017). https://www.datamation.com/big-data/big-data-challenges.html
17. Kitzes, J., Turek, D., Deniz, F. (eds.): The Practice of Reproducible Research: Case Studies and Lessons from the Data-Intensive Sciences. Oakland, CA: University of California Press, CA (2018). https://www.practicereproducibleresearch.org/#
18. Earnshaw, R.A.: Chapter 3 in State of the Art in Digital Media and Applications, pp. 21–28. Springer, Cham, Switzerland (2017). https://www.springer.com/gb/book/9783319614083